Letters from a Nut

Ted L. Nancy

EBURY
PRESS

First published in Great Britain in 2003

17

Copyright © 1997 Ted L. Nancy's Hand-Dipped Productions
Introduction copyright © 1997 Jerry Seinfeld

First published by Avon Books, Inc.

Ebury Press, an imprint of Random House,
20 Vauxhall Bridge Road, London SW1V 2SA

Random House Australia (Pty) Limited
20 Alfred Street, Milsons Point, Sydney,
New South Wales 2061, Australia

Random House New Zealand Limited
18 Poland Road, Glenfield, Auckland 10, New Zealand

Random House South Africa (Pty) Limited
Isle of Houghton, Corner of Boundary Road & Carse O'Gowrie,
Houghton 2198, South Africa

The Random House Group Limited Reg. No. 954009

www.randomhouse.co.uk

Penguin Random House is committed to a sustainable future for
our business, our readers and our planet. This book is made from
Forest Stewardship Council® certified paper.

Printed and bound in Great Britain by Clays Ltd, St Ives plc

A CIP catalogue record for this book is available from the British Library.

Cover designed by Keenan

ISBN 9780091895365

Dedicated to Rita, Marty, and Alan
I'm proud and happy to be the end table in this living room set

Also dedicated to
Marilyn, Leonard, Lynn, Jenna, Dylan,
Marla, and Stuart

Acknowledgments

thanks to Lou Aronica, Patricia Lande Grader, Andrea Sinert, Dan Strone, Debra Bard, Budd Friedman, and Jerry Seinfeld.

and to Phyllis Murphy, who was there at the beginning when I opened a bag of Fritos and said, "These are all curled, crunchy, and salty. I'm going to write to Fritos and tell them about it." And she said, "I think you should."

Introduction

ℳy first contact with Mr. Ted Nancy was the night of August 30, 1995. I went to a friend's house to watch the Jerry Lewis Labor Day Telethon, which I watch every year. There were a few other people there, and as we were enjoying the program, I noticed a handful of letters sitting on the coffee table. I read one, and then another, and then another. I began to laugh out loud at the letters, and just as much at the responses from the various businesses and corporations that followed each one. Then I started reading the letters to my friends, and the next thing I know, the whole room was laughing and having a wonderful time. I stopped reading only when Jerry Lewis sang "When You Walk Through a Storm." I never miss that part every year. It's one of my favorite things.

Anyway, one thing I know as a comedian is that it's very rare for people to laugh out loud at television or the printed word even though they may be enjoying it very much. But the people in that den were really laughing. Believe me, I know laughs, and these were real big show business laughs. I thought, *I don't know what this is, but it's some pretty powerful stuff.*

There was just one strange thing. There was this one fellow in the room who just kind of nodded approvingly as each letter was read. He didn't seem irritated, nor did he seem particularly impressed. He was just sort of sitting back, taking the whole thing in.

I have learned over the years how when funny people see their work appreciated, it's something like when parents watch their children playing. They may not be involved, but there's this detached pride in the joy that they feel indirectly responsible for. That was the look on that man's face that night. I guess I didn't realize it at the time, but I am convinced to this day that that man was the real Ted L. Nancy.

When I left, I asked the host if I could borrow the letters. I didn't know what I was going to do with them. I think I really just wanted to read them again. So I took them home, and over the next couple of weeks, read them again to various people I know whose senses of humor have been rigorously developed to professional strength.

I must, by the way, mention if you should find yourself in possession of this book, one of the great joys of it is definitely reading the letters out loud. And always be careful to point out when something is in parentheses. The careful use of the parenthetical phrase is my favorite aspect of the Ted Nancy writing style.

Anyway, everyone's reaction was the same as the night of the telethon. You cannot not laugh at these letters. So I called my friend, whose house it was, and asked him if he could get any more of the letters. He said, "Sure, there's lots more." Then I called my literary agent, Dan Strone of the William Morris Agency, an extremely charming and well dressed man and, more importantly, one of the smartest guys in show business. I said, "Dan, I have a bunch of letters here that I think could be some kind of book if you could get enough of them." So Dan got an outfit together and a lunch was arranged.

I had now taken on the role of a Clark Kent figure. I may not have been Superman himself, but it became known that I was able to contact him. There wasn't much else I had to do after that. When you give something good to Dan Strone, it's like handling the ball off to Gale Sayers. You just know it's going places.

As far as Ted L. Nancy himself goes, I'm really still pretty much in the dark about him. From his Vegas shrimp costume to his dog play, "Cinnamon, A Life in Progress," to his lost bag of otter hair, it's hard to figure out what's driving this guy. I will say that Ted L. Nancy definitely possesses many of the qualities I consider essential for a good life. He enjoys the simple things, like fine busboy service, Bon Ami cleanser, and steamboats. He is extremely courteous and complimentary to his correspondents and will go to any length to find a kind word to say. "You make great horseradish sauce," he writes the Excalibur hotel.

On the other hand, he does not travel well or easily. Always requiring special arrangements or permission to be made in advance for his various costumes, furniture, draperies, and vending machines. Mr. Nancy is also apparently a gifted and versatile live performer, offering many types of freak and celebrity impersonations. Unfortunately, the shows are inevitably derailed by poor advance booking commitments.

I guess I would like to say that in many ways Ted Nancy is a lot like you and me. We all have peculiar problems and often have to deal with faceless strangers to resolve them. But it's just not true. Ted Nancy is not like you and me. Nobody has problems like this guy. Nobody travels with a Prussian military sword and then loses it. Nobody is writing fan letters to Max Schmeling. Nobody is going to hotels asking if they can wet the bed and bring their own ice machines. And nobody, but nobody, is in contact with a real African king trying to locate his girlfriend's lost mail.

But this guy is. And I knew from the beginning that I had to do everything I could to let as many people as possible read the hilarious truth about what has been going on inside the mailbox of Ted L. Nancy, whoever he may be.

Jerry Seinfeld

HeLp Me!

560 North Moorpark RD.
236
Thousand Oaks, CA 91360

July 12, 1995

MANAGER
RITZ CARLTON HOTEL
160 East Pearson Street
Chicago, Ill. 60611

Dear Sir:

I wanted to know if you possibly found a Prussian military
sword that I think I may have left in your hotel restaurant the
night of Saturday, July 7th?   I was in your men's room when I
loosened the sword to go to the restroom.

I am with a traveling group and was in costume the night I used
your restroom. When I was washing my hands I noticed that your
paper towel rack was empty. With wet hands I went over to a
stall to get some tissue (Your hand dryer was not working!)

I had to loosen my trousers to use the facility. In doing so I
loosened the sword (actually took it off) and somehow forgot to
put it back on when I pulled my trousers up again. That's how I
think the sword may be in your restroom.

The sword is a standard size sword in a jewled (fake) encrusted
sheath. The sheath is crushed velvet (also fake). It was on a
sword belt, size 36. It has no value other than as part of a
costume I wear.

Please contact me at the following address:

Ted L. Nancy
560 N. Moorpark Rd #236
Thousand Oaks, CA 91360

Thank you very much for your help in this matter, Ritz Carlton.

P.S. You have great sea bass!

THE RITZ-CARLTON
CHICAGO
A Four Seasons Hotel

Mr. Ted NANCY   26JULY95
560 North Moorpark Rd. #236
Thousand Oaks, Ca.   91360

Dear Sir:

Upon receiving your letter on 17JULY95, the Security Department started investigating your loss of the Prussian Military Sword.

Sir, the Security Department is sorry to inform you that we were unable to locate your sword.

Sir, if you have any questions or further information, please give me a call at 1(312)266-1000 Ext#4040. I would be happy to assist you.

John ALMANZA
Ritz-Carlton Hotel
Security Department
160 East Pearson Street
Chicago, Il.   60611

EXECUTIVE OFFICES
NORDSTROM DEPARTMENT STORES
1501 Fifth Ave
Seattle, WA 98101   Aug 4, 1995

Dear Nordstrom Dept Stores.

I am a regular shopper at your Nordstroms store in Glendale. In
the last few weeks I have noticed that a new mannequin you have
out in the store looks just like my deceased neighbor. I have
passed this mannequin from many directions and the resemblance is
uncanny. In every way - nose, cheekbones, hair, etc. Look at it
from any angle. It looks like the neighbor I was friendly with.
Even the clothes that the mannequin was wearing is the kind of
lightweight windbreaker jacket my neighbor would wear. It is
UNBELIEVABLE that this mannequin looks so much like my neighbor.

Is it possible to buy this mannequin (after its use) so I may
present it to my neighbor's family? They would think this would
be a VERY sentimental gesture. I think his co-workers would also
like to have him remembered, so having him "there" would be good,
therapeutic behavior for all.

I was told to write to your store's HEADQUARTERS OFFICE after I
inquired about buying this mannequin to the saleslady (Very,
courteous, I may add.) She suggested that only the stores main
office could assist me in this purchase. But she was very helpful
with my socks purchase.

Thank you, Nordstrom, for being a store that cares about its
customers. I am a long time shopper. I keep lots of things in
your Nordstrom bags. Fishing gear, etc. I have a garage full of
Nordstrom bags full of old shoes, wire hangers, etc. That's how I
know I've been to your store so much. Let me know about the
mannequin. This family is in some need of good loving. This will
help!

Sincerely,

Ted L. Nancy
560 N. Moorpark Rd. #236
Thousand Oaks, Ca 91360

NORDSTROM

August 14, 1995

Mr. Ted L. Nancy
560 N. Moorpark Road, #236
Thousand Oaks, CA 91360

Dear Mr. Nancy:

Yours is one of the most interesting requests I have ever received. Candidly, I can't imagine any family who has lost a loved one wanting to see a mannequin that resembles that person.

Of course, we want to respond to our customers as positively as possible, but we definitely do not sell display materials while they are being used by the company. I see no reason why (when it comes time for a change of mannequins) that we wouldn't sell it to you at the same price we would get from our normal resources.

If you should be interested in that, simply talk to our store manager there at Glendale, Diane Kantor, and she will let you know when the time comes. Unfortunately, mannequins are used for a number of years before they are phased out.

Sincerely,

Bruce A. Nordstrom

BAN/ks

cc: Diane Kantor, Store Manager, Glendale
       Roland Thiele, Corporate Display Manager

NORDSTROM

August 24, 1995

Mr. Ted L. Nancy
560 N. Moorpark Road, #236
Thousand Oaks, CA 91360

Dear Mr. Nancy:

Your letter was forwarded to me by Mr. Bruce Nordstrom and I am aware of your request for a particular mannequin resembling a deceased friend. After reading your letter I was somewhat perplexed as to which mannequin you were talking about as our store does not use Male mannequins in our display area, including the window and departments.

As Mr. Nordstrom shared with you, we generally do not sell display materials while they are being used; however, I would be more than happy to work with you once we are able to isolate which mannequin this could be and once it is phased out.

Mr. Nancy, please do not hesitate to call me and hopefully together we can decipher exactly which mannequin you are referring to. I can be reached at (818)502-9922 or you may leave a message with our Store Secretary, Amy Tiner.

Sincerely,

NORDSTROM

Diane Kantor.

Diane Kantor
Store Manager

DK/at

cc: Bruce Nordstrom,Director
     Roland Thiele, Corporate Display Manager

NORDSTROM

200 W. Broadway
Glendale, CA 91204-1332

Mr. Ted L. Nancy
560 N. Moorpark road, #236
Thousand Oaks, CA 91360

Ted L. Nancy
560 N. Moorpark Rd., #236
Thousand Oaks, CA 91360

July 10th, 1995

MR. ALBERT H. MEYER, PRESIDENT
AMERICAN SEATING COMPANY
901 Broadway
Grand Rapids, Michigan
49504

Dear Mr. Meyer:

I had a seating question and I was referred to you because I
understand you manufacture stadium and arena seating. My
question:

When entering or exiting a seat in a stadium which is the proper
side to face the person sitting down? Rear to them or crotch to
them?

I am always at a quandry when this problem comes up. To hence:
last week at a sporting event I had to leave my seat. There were
a row of people - ALL FROM THE SAME FAMILY - that were sitting
down the row. I exited my seat, stood up and faced away from
this family. Then I moved down the row realizing my buttocks
were not 2 inches from this whole guy's family. I had shown an
entire family my rear end!   But then again If I had turned
around and moved down the aisel THAT WAY, wouldn't that be worse?

Stadium seating is the only situation in life where you can show
whole rows of people your butt or crotch. And it's acceptable! .

Can something be done about this seating? Should the rows be
changed? I suggest a single row straight up to the top. You
walk into the stadium you simply find your seat number and go up
until you get it.

Question: Is there a gracious way to exit?
Thank you, Sir, for your response.

Ted L. Nancy

☆AMERICANSEATING

August 3, 1995

Ted L. Nancy
560 N. Moorpark Rd., #236
Thousand Oaks, CA 91360

Dear Mr. Nancy:

Your letter on crotch or butt first was most interesting. In fact, in all 38 years which I have been in this business it is probably the most interesting question I have ever been asked. I have shared your letter with numerous of my colleagues, and they have also found it most interesting.

But alas, we have no good answer. Your idea of a single chair has merit, but unfortunately would greatly reduce the number of chairs which could be put in the building.

The only suggestion we could come up with is for you to come early before anyone has arrived, stay in your seat for the entire time, and wait until everyone else has gone before leaving. This, of course, could cause an even more embarrassing problem.

If you come up with any solutions we would welcome hearing from you.

Sincerely,

Albert H. Meyer

American Seating Company
901 Broadway, N.W.
Grand Rapids, Michigan 49504-4499
Telephone 616 / 732-6600

Printed on Recycled Paper

560 North Moorpark Road #236
Thousand Oaks, CA. 91360
Sept. 10, 1995

GENERAL MANAGER
LUXOR HOTEL & CASINO
3900 Las Vegas Blvd. South
Las Vegas, NV 89119-1000

Dear Luxor Hotel & Casino General Manager,

I am building a house that's in the same shape as your hotel and
wonder if it would be ok if I came by your hotel and took some
pictures of the outside?   I think your hotel is the perfect
design for my house. I would stand on the far corners of each
sidewalk and take a few pictures.

This is a private house; 2 bedroom, 2 1/2 bath; family room,
breakfast nook, den, patio, dog walk in the back. There are
some orange trees. And a big front yard. This is not a
commercial venture. I am not building a hotel or gas station or
mini mart. I am not building a place like your Hotel where
there is wear and tear on the carpet. It is just a house for
myself.   I was told to write to the Hotel General Manager when
I inquired about this to the HOUSEKEEPING DEPARTMENT. They
directed me to you.

I wanted to come by and take a few pictures of the outside of
your Luxor Hotel. One picture would be of your long gray wall.
The other is also of the wall but on the other side facing the
other street. There's some bushes there. I would use a
Polaroid. I was told I needed to get permission from you.

Thank you, Luxor. I have long admired your hotel. I have
always thought it would be a perfect design for a house.
Although I would do it a different color. I'm thinking beige.
And not that glint. I love the slanted walls!

So...please let me know If it would be ok if I took some outside
pictures of your hotel. I will make little commotion as I would
just take the pictures and leave. My car is across the street.
This would help the stucco and plasterer guy on my house.
Or
If you already have a picture of the outside of your hotel that
you could send me, that would be ok. Anything that shows those
outside walls off. Thanks very much.

Respectfully,

Ted L. Nancy

Circus Circus Enterprises, Inc.

TONY ALAMO
Senior Vice President

September 18, 1995

Mr. Ted L. Nancy
560 North Moorpark Road, #236
Thousand Oaks, CA   91360

Dear Mr. Nancy:

I am in receipt of your recent letter.

It is perfectly all right for you to take exterior pictures of the Luxor Hotel and Casino during your next visit to Las Vegas as long as you do not jeopardize the safety of yourself, the Luxor or any guests of the Luxor.   If you are unsure if you are allowed to be in a particular location during your picture session, please contact Andy Vanyo, our Chief of Security.

Good luck with your house!

Sincerely,

Tony Alamo
Senior Vice-President

TA:ps
file

Copy: Andy Vanyo, Chief of Security

Mr. Gordon Besher, PRESIDENT
Bon Ami Cleanser Company
Kansas City, Mo.
64101 - 1200   July 11, 1995
1995

Dear Mr Gordon Besher,

I think that's your name. Your signature is muffled on the side
of my Bon Ami cleanser. It could say Gordon Burkar the third,
so my apologies to you and others in your family that may have
your name.

I am writing to you because on the side of the product (Bon Ami
Kitchen and Bath Cleanser) it says- followed by your signature -

"I personally warrant this product to be of quality and
integrity. If you are not satisfied, please return to me with
your comments for refund and postage. We wish to continue
earning your confidence." Signed Gordon Bruckar the third
(possibly the fourth).

These are your exact words. So, my question to you, Sir, is
what do you mean by this product being of integrity?

Don't get me wrong, your product is very, very good. I have
cleaned a lot of things with Bon Ami over the years. It is the
best at stains I have ever seen since Bab-O. The "quality" is
there. Just what is the "integrity?"

So, these are my comments. I look forward to hearing from you.

I will continue to use Bon Ami.

Your loyal customer, (No more stains!)

Ted L. Nancy
Ted L. Nancy

Faultless Starch / Bon Ami Company

Gordon T. Beaham, III
Chairman of the Board
President

July 18, 1995

Mr. Ted L. Nancy
560 N. Moorpark Road., Apt 236
Thousand Oaks, CA 91360

Dear Mr. Nancy:

Thank you for your good letter of July 11. I agree -- my signature isn't all that clear, is it?

Integrity is a great concept, isn't it? Webster's Dictionary defines the word as follows: 1: firm adherence to a code of especially moral or artistic values: <u>INCORRUPTIBILITY</u>   2: an unimpaired condition: <u>SOUNDNESS</u>   3: the quality or state of being complete or undivided: <u>COMPLETENESS</u>   Synonym -- see <u>HONESTY</u>

When we bought Bon Ami® in 1971 it had been through 5 or 6 successive companies since the early '50's. It had a bad reputation with the trade because advertising was promised but not often delivered. It had a formula more expensive than competition. It's main reason for being, from the start, was to clean fine hard surfaces without damaging them. Harsh cleansers frequently took the shine off of bathtub surfaces over time, for example. Bon Ami's original advertising, back in the early 1900's, used the baby chick with the saying "Hasn't scratched yet!®" because, apparently, when a chick hatches out of an egg it has enough food in it from the yolk that it doesn't have to hurry out right away and start scratching for food.

So we want Bon Ami to always adhere to it's prime purpose, cleaning without scratching. It doesn't have perfume or coloring, which are really not necessary. It doesn't have chlorine bleach because the bleach can further etch into the scratches harsh cleansers make.

MAILING ADDRESS, PLANT & LABORATORY: 1025 W. 8th STREET • KANSAS CITY, MO 64101-1200 • (816) 842-2939
CORPORATE OFFICE: 510 WALNUT STREET • KANSAS CITY, MO 64106-1209 • (816) 842-1230
FAX: OFFICE (816) 842-3417 • PLANT (816) 842-0215 • LAB (816) 421-3052 • TELEX: 42272BONAMI KSC

I hope that that answers your question for you. A further answer might come from the dust cover of Jack Hawley's new book, *Reawakening The Spirit In Work -- the Power of Dharmic Management*. I attached a xerox of its cover and dust jacket.

I had to admit that I had to look up the word "Dharmic". I like it. That's what we're trying to do here. But I don't intend to put that word on the can.

I hope that this answers your question satisfactorily for you. Thank you again for your good letter, for your loyalty, and your continued use of Bon Ami. I will pass your letter among those who make it, knowing that it will make them each just a little prouder of the job he or she is doing.

I'm enclosing a little booklet on our company for your information. My best wishes to you.

Sincerely yours,

Gordon T. Beaham, III

GTB,III:kc
enclosures

No Chlorine, Phosphates, Perfume or Dye

bon ami

KITCHEN & BATH CLEANSER

560 N. Moorpark Rd., Apt 236
Thousand Oaks, CA 91360

Jul 22, 1995

HAWAIIAN TROPIC
TANNING RESEARCH LABS INC.
RON RICE BEACH PROD.
Box 5111
Daytona Beach, Fla.   32118

Dear Hawaiian Tropic Tanning Lotion,

Recently I wore a tank top with holes in it to an outdoor concert
on a hot sunny day. You guessed it - I got a real severe tan.

So I picked out some Hawaiian Tropic Tanning Lotion to even out
the color of my tan. I rubbed it on the white spots as the
directions said. Let me tell you it looks great!!! One
problem...

I can't get the copper tan color off the palms of my hands. My
palms are tan. I look like a giant toffee man. With nuts.
(ha ha). From a distance people can't tell if I'm coming or
going.

I was thinking of trying to get it off with acetone or acetaline
but I'm not sure which is correct. What do you suggest? Any job
openings?

Eagerly awaiting your reply.

Ted L. Nancy,
Consultant

WORLD CLASS SUNCARE

August 2, 1995

Ted L. Nancy
560 N. Moorpark Rd. Apt. 236
Thousand Oaks, CA 91360

Dear Mr. Nancy:

We were sorry to hear of the problem you had with a Hawaiian Tropic self tanning product.

The active ingredient, dihydroxyacetone, or DHA, reacts with the amino acids in the skin to creat the tanned appearance. Exfoliation of the affected skin layers is the way this "tan" fades. In fact, you probably will have faded by the time you receive this letter.

You can try to speed it along by scrubbing your skin with a wash cloth or loufa sponge, but this doesn't work for everybody. I haven't heard of removing the color with acetone or acetaline. After any future applications be sure to wash your palms right away to prevent discoloration.

The only job openings we have right now are for warehouse personnel and quality control inspectors.

Thank you for your letter and we hope you continue to use and enjoy Hawaiian Tropic suncare products.

Sincerely,

Mary Kuffner
Marketing Services Representative
Tanning Research Laboratories, Inc.

encl.

560 N. Moorpark Rd., Apt 236
Thousand Oaks, CA 91360

Dec 14, 1995

MS. Mary Kuffner
Marketing Service Representative
HAWAIIAN TROPIC
Tanning Research Laboratories, Inc.
P.O. Box 5111
Daytona, Beach, Fla
32118-5111

Dear MS. Kuffner:

Thank you for writing me back and helping me with my Hawaiian Tan
problem. It was a mess! I am sorry it took me so long to write
back to you. I have been traveling as part of a semi-small group.

You mentioned in your letter that there are job openings available
at Hawaiian Tropic: Warehouse personnel and quality control
inspectors. I would like to apply for the job of Quality Control
Inspector. I'd rather inspect something then move something. Let
somebody else do it, I'll take a look at it and make sure they did
it right. I'm always checking things out. Friends say, "Ted, you
should be a quality control inspector." One question: If you are
looking for a quality control inspector, who is inspecting the
product NOW?

Please send me info on applying for a job at Hawaiian Tropic.
Thanks for everything and also your samples. They came in handy!
(One lasts through the whole movie)!

Respectfully,

Ted L. Nancy

WORLD CLASS SUNCARE

HAWAIIAN Tropic ®

February 27, 1996

Ted L. Nancy
560 N. Moorpark Road Apt. 236
Thousand Oaks, CA 91360

Dear Mr. Nancy:

Thank you for your interest in applying for employment with this company. Since your first letter to us, the position of Quality Control Inspector has been filled. Our corporate policy is to only accept applications for specific positions that are open. Currently there are no openings.

We would be happy to consider your application for a specific opening in the future. Please send future inquiries regarding employment to the attention of the Personnel Department.

Sincerely,

Mary Kuffner

Mary Kuffner
Marketing Services Representative
Tanning Research Laboratories, Inc.

Ted L. Nancy
560 No. Moorpark Rd. #236
Thousand Oaks, CA. 91360

SECRETARY MIKE ESPY
SECRETARY OF AGRICULTURE
The Mall, 12th & 14th Sts,
Washington, D.C. 20250   12/7/95

Dear Secretary Espy:

I'm in a jam, Sir. (Hence the top of the stationary). I told
everybody at work that you would be our speaker at our
organization of tennis shoe retailers. I have been an admirer of
you and your leadership and thought you would be the most
appropriate one to raise the moral of our sales force. We cover
the western United States in athletic shoe sales.

Is there any way that you could speak at this meeting? (Late
February). It would mean a lot for our down trodden and
depressed salesman to hear a speaker of your wisdom. A leader
who has led the people of America in a favorable manner. I want
these men to hear a real Secretary.

These salesmen need to hear a leader of your wisdom. A leader
that can lift them out of the temporary stupor they are in. This
was once a sales force that could outsell any athletic shoe
manufacturer in the Pacific Northwest. Now they are completely
depressed over coming in fifth (out of 8) in the recent
"Saleabration '95 Expo."

Naturally, everyone is so excited at the prospect of you being
there. I could lose my job if you're a no-show! Thank you in
advance for your reply. Do you do these type of speaking
engagements? If you can't show can I get a picture of you to
have for our meeting?

With Respect, Sir,

Ted L. Nancy
Chair Committee
Saleabration Expo '96

DEPARTMENT OF AGRICULTURE
OFFICE OF THE SECRETARY
WASHINGTON, D. C. 20250

December 18, 1995

Mr. Ted L. Nancy
560 No. Moorpark Road #236
Thousand Oaks, CA 91360

Dear Mr. Nancy:

Your letter requesting Secretary Mike Espy to speak at the Saleabration Expo '96 was received in our office on December 12, 1995. Mr. Espy left the position of Secretary of Agriculture in December of 1994; therefore, if you would like him to address your group, you will have to contact him at his home address.

If I can be of any further assistance, do not hesitate to contact me.

Sincerely,

Mary Hedrick

Mary F. Hedrick
Travel/Speech Coordinator

560 North Moorpark Rd. #236
Thousand Oaks, CA 91360

LOST & FOUND DEPT.
BROWN PALACE HOTEL
321 17th Street
Denver, CO 80202   Sep 14, 1995

Dear Lost & Found Dept.:

When visiting your hotel the afternoon of last Saturday, I bit
down onto some crackers.   Later on, after I woke up, I realized
I had lost a tooth. Did anyone find a tooth in your hotel?
I'll describe it. It is a small hard whitish object. The size
of a piece of corn. It has a rippled top; speck of silver
embedded in the top.

If anyone has found this tooth I would like to come and pick it
up. I do not want somebody else's tooth. I have had that
happen before. PLEASE DO NOT MAIL IT!   I do not want to lose
it again.

I believe my tooth could be somewhere in the sundries shop,
probably by the front, or it could be in the lobby on the floor
somewhere in the back. I don't know where I lost it but I do
know it was not in my head when I left your hotel last Saturday.
Thanks for getting back to me on this.

Respectfully,

Ted L. Nancy

The Second Century

17 October 1995

Mr. Ted L. Nancy
560 North Moorpark Road #236
Thousand Oaks, CA   91360

Dear Sir:

In response to your letter of 17 September, we proceeded at once to check the areas mentioned. Also, we have checked our Lost and Found records, and have monitored items turned in since then. We have failed to find your missing tooth.

Such a loss is regrettable. No doubt, it is an inconvenience to you. Although I do not believe it likely that the tooth will be returned to us this long after the loss, let me assure you that we will keep record of your letter, and will let you know if the tooth is returned.

If I can help you in any other way, please let me know.

Yours, in Service,

Stan Roebuck
Director of Loss Prevention

560 North Moorpark Rd. #236
Thousand Oaks, CA 91360

Mr. Stan Roebuck
Director Of Loss Prevention
BROWN PALACE HOTEL
321 17th Street
Denver, CO 80202   Oct 23, 1995

Dear Mr. Roebuck:

Thank you very much for the time and effort you put into finding
my lost tooth. Yes, the loss is regrettable.   Although you did
not find it, I want to tell you how impressed I was of your
dedication to the Brown Palace and their guests. Your diligent
search did not go unnoticed.

A copy of this letter has been placed in my file and a record of
it logged for future use. It has been shared internally.

In addition, I am <u>Singling You Out</u> for <u>Exemplary Service</u> and a
letter to that effect has been sent to the President of the
Brown Palace Hotel to let him know how courteous, professional,
and dedicated their fine Director Of Loss Prevention is to their
customer's needs. Your attention to this matter is outstanding!

For your dedicated service I am wondering if you can accept a
gift? I would like to reward you for your diligence. Does the
Brown Palace allow you to accept the generosities of another?
Please get back to me on this. It is important that I know that
you know that we both know that you were thanked.

I anxiously await your reply concerning the gift.
(Re: Cinnamon)

Respectfully,

Ted L. Nancy

Ted L. Nancy

Certificate
of
Excellence

Awarded to: MR. STAN ROEBUCK

THE BROWN PALACE HOTEL

For: **Diligent service in trying to locate Ted L. Nancy's <u>tooth</u>**

(Small hard whitish object; size of a piece of corn. Rippled top, speck of silver. Some food in it.)

On This Day, 26 August 1996

Signed,

Ted L. Nancy

_____

Ted L. Nancy

560 No. Moorpark Rd. #236
Thousand Oaks, CA. 91360

Oct 23, 1995

LOST & FOUND DEPT
COLORADO BELLE HOTEL & CASINO
P.O. Box 77000
Laughlin, NV 89028

Dear Lost & Found Department:

I was told to write to you on this matter after I inquired about
it at your hotel.

While visiting the Colorado Belle recently I stopped to use the
facilities. After being distracted in the commode due to
influences that were not your fault I believe I accidentally
left behind a small Altar to my deceased neighbor: a lock of
hair, photo, scentbag, toenails, breath pad.   It was in a
container with a strand of ribbon around it. It had a birch
smell to it. (Not the root beer!) It was in commode #2. (I
think).

I am now wondering if it it was thrown away. Could you please
tell me if the hotel has found this Altar?   If not, do you
think I should search your trash?   Many things have been in the
trash and retrieved. It is very important! The box alone is
worth at least the box. The photo has no value except to me.
Although you may enjoy it.

I must hear from you regarding this find. This Altar is my
neighbor's worship bag. He needs some peace!   Thank you,
Colorado Belle. You are a hotel that allows your customers some
leeway now and then. Especially when it comes to your trash!

Respectfully,

Ted L. Nancy

P.S. The Bus Staff should be complimented and singled out!

COLORADO BELLE
HOTEL & CASINO
P.O. BOX 77000 • LAUGHLIN, NEVADA 89028
Nautically Appointed Rooms and Suites, 2 Pools and Spa, 60,000 Sq. Ft. Gaming Area,
Over 1,500 Slots, "21", Craps, Keno, Roulette, Poker, 6 Distinctive Dining Areas,
#230 Arcade, Gift Shops, Candy Shoppe.
For Reservations Call 1-800-47-RIVER within the Continental U.S.
or Dial Direct (702) 298-4000

11/5

Mr. Nancy,
I'm sorry but we haven't been
able to find your altar. All of our
trash goes to a public dump ground
in Laughlin.   Sincerely,
                    Wilmet
                    Lost & Found.

Post Card

LAUGHLIN
NV
NOV 1995
PM LTR 1
6760521

U.S. POSTAGE
≈ 020
PEACE
POSTAGE
HERE

Ted L. Nancy
560 N. Moorpark Rd #236
Thousand Oaks, Ca.
91360

560 No. Moorpark Rd. #236
Thousand Oaks, CA 91360

1/3/96

Mr. Steven Frautschi
Executive Officer, Physics Dept
CALIFORNIA INSTITUTE OF TECHNOLOGY
1201 East California Blvd.
Pasadena, Ca. 91125

Dear Mr. Frautschi,

Doesn't it make sense to you, that if you weighed 150 pounds, and
you could lift 300 pounds, you should be able to fly by sitting on
a chair and lifting yourself up? How come this doesn't work? The
best I can do is jiggle the chair a bit. Am I doing something
wrong? My neighbor said it has something to do with gravity, and
it's like a physics optical illusion. I think I'm just doing
something wrong. Does it matter if the chair is backless or has
armrests?

I was told to write to you, that you could help me with the
answer. They directed me here. They said you could help me with
this problem for our studies. Thank you very much, Sir, for your
reply. I hope to excel in Physics some day like you. I think I'm
doing "ok" now.

Sincerely,

Ted L. Nancy

1/18/96

Dear Mr. Nancy,

I'll attempt to answer your query of 1/3/96.

Gravity will always pull you down, unless there is a supporting force holding you up. Normally the floor, or a chair, supplies this supporting force. By applying an _extra_ force, eg with your legs when jumping or with your arms pushing down against a firm support such as armrests, you can jump up temporarily into the air (it's easier to do with your legs – they are thicker and stronger than your arms). But once airborn, gravity pulls you down again unless you can find a way to keep pushing down on the air. To apply your strength you need something to push against, and it's hard to get enough air to push against. If you were outfitted with wings with a large surface area, _then_ you might have enough air to push against and you might be able to fly briefly as in sail planing (or the man who powered a winged bicycle across the English Channel using his leg muscles). But that's hard – the wings have to be very lightweight and well-engineered.

I hope I've answered at least part of your question.

Steven Frautschi

CALIFORNIA INSTITUTE OF TECHNOLOGY
PASADENA, CALIFORNIA 91125

PASADENA, CA 91
PM
11 JAN
1996

VIA AIR MAIL

Mr. Ted L. Nancy
560 No. Moorpark Rd. #236
Thousand Oaks, CA 91360

DREAMS

The Earl Of Sandwich Once Said...

"There is no future without
todays dreams. Now bring me
another falafel."

(Two years before his discovery)

Ted L. Nancy
560 North Moorpark Road
Suite 236
Thousand Oaks, Ca 91360

Aug 3, 1995

GENERAL MANAGER
WHISKY PETES HOTEL AND CASINO
P.O. Box 19129
Jean, NV 89019

Dear Whisky Pete's General Manager:

I am contemplating opening a gift shop/eatery near the
Nevada/California border. I want to call this place "WHISKY
PATS." "This will be a VERY SMALL trailer type operation. I hope
that my name - "WHISKY PATS" - does not interfere with your name -
"WHISKY PETES." Although slightly similar, we offer a different
product. While you have gambling, liquor, and buffets. Whisky
Pats will offer just a regular menu.   We will not have gambling
on the premises, but we will be selling tiny slot machines, poker
games, and dealers aprons in our gift area. We will have a full
line of gaming cards and dice from various casinos for sale.
(Some Whisky Petes).

You WILL be able to SEE the WHISKY PATS sign from some of your
guest rooms. (If curtains are open).   Our sign will not be
similar at all. While yours says - "WHISKY PETES" - my sign has
"PAT" instead of "PETE." The "WHISKY" is the same. But it will
blink out of unison with yours. Your sign blinks, then ours.
So...when your sign blinks then goes dark - my sign blinks. When
mine is dark - your's blinks. It will be two different signs
blinking one right after each other. (I may have music).

So...It is my contention that the name Whisky Pats is OK with you
and that I will NOT HAVE any problems should they come up with the
possible similarity of the two names.

I have respected your establishment for a long time and have been
a good customer there. I will continue to frequent "Whisky
Petes." When I get off work at "Whisky Pats", I will run over to
"Whisky Petes" for a quick game of keno and some craps.

Thanks for everything. I look forward to being your neighbor.

Ted L. Nancy
For Whisky Pats

PRIMADONNA
Resorts, Inc.

P.O. Box 95997

Las Vegas, Nevada 89193-5997

August 10, 1995   (702) 382-1212

<u>Certified Mail -- Return Receipt Requested</u>

Mr. Ted L. Nancy
560 North Moorpark Road
Suite 236
Thousand Oaks, CA 91360

      Re: Protection of Name Symbols & Likenesses of Whiskey Pete's/Whisky
           Pats" _____

Dear Nancy:

      On August 9, 1995, I received your letter dated August 3, 1995, to the
"General Manager of Whiskey Pete's Hotel & Casino." I have been asked to
respond.

      While we appreciate your request to share protected names, logos, likeness and
symbols, we must refuse and reject your request in the most absolute terms.
Primadonna has spent tremendous sums to promote the "Whiskey Pete's" name.
The name has tremendous commercial value and belongs exclusively to Primadonna.
Primadonna has also taken necessary steps to legally protect this name and many
other names, devices, merchandising, logos and related intellectual property rights.

      Accordingly, we must reject your proposal to share the "Whiskey Pete's" or
"Whisky Pats" name in any way and demand that you not pursue this matter further.
If you do, we will be forced to pursue all legal avenues available to protect our rights
to this important name.

                    Sincerely,

                    Greg Jensen
                    General Counsel

cc: William Paulos
    Arnie Fleischman

BOURBON JOE'S

"Stateline's Newest Place To Go"

560 North Moorpark Road #236
Thousand Oaks, California
91360
(Mailing address)

MR. GREG JENSEN
WHISKEY PETE'S CASINO
P.O. BOX 95997
Las Vegas, Nevada
89193-5997   Sept. 6, 1995

Dear Mr. Jensen,

Ok, ok I will not call myself "Whiskey Pats." I can understand
you came up with this name first. I have always admired that
name, "Whiskey Pete's." Whenever I have passed the "Whiskey
Pete's" sign I have always enjoyed viewing it. Whoever came up
with that name hit a bingo. So consider this letter my word, my
bond, my chattel in promising you that I have abandoned the idea
of calling my business "Whisky Pats." (I had thought about
putting an "e" in "Whisky" but decided against it). As far as I
am concerned "Whisky Pats" is no more, finis, the end. "Whiskey
Pete's" can have full use of the area for their sign blinking.

Please be my guest when we have our grand opening of "Bourbon
Joe's." Our business will not in anyway interfere with yours.
While you have gambling, buffets and entertainment, ours will
have SOME food but not buffet style; you pay for everything ala
carte. (Except spaghetti on Wednesdays). Please let me know If
there is ANY problem with my name - "Bourbon Joe's." I believe
I have come up with this name on my own, without any outside
influence. I would like to call my mini-giftshop, sandwich
place, gamblers den "BOURBON JOE'S" without any worry from you.
Please let me know If I may proceed. Thank you.

Finally your neighbor
I love your Sign!

Ted L. Nancy

Ted L. Nancy
For Bourbon Joe's

STILL WAITING FOR REPLY!

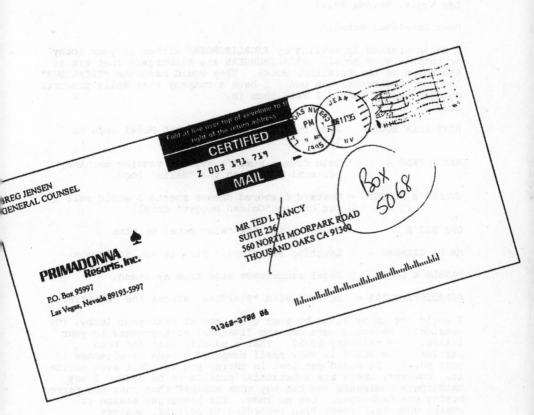

GREG JENSEN
GENERAL COUNSEL

PRIMADONNA Resorts, Inc.

P.O. Box 95997
Las Vegas, Nevada 89193-5997

MR TED L NANCY
SUITE 236
560 NORTH MOORPARK ROAD
THOUSAND OAKS CA 91360

Box 5068

91360-3788 04

560 North Moorpark Road #236
Thousand Oaks, CA. 91360
Aug 23, 1995

EXECUTIVE OFFICE
EXCALIBUR HOTEL & CASINO
P.O. Box 96778
Las Vegas, Nevada 89193

Dear Excalibur Hotel,

I am interested in selling my EXCALIBURGERS either in your lobby
or outside your hotel. EXCALIBURGERS are hamburgers that are in
the shape of the Excalibur Hotel. They would have the "EXCALIBUR"
logo on them across the bun. I have a company that sells products
related to the hotels I sell them in.
<u>Like:</u>

RIVI AREA RUGS -   Area rugs with the "Riviera" Hotel logo on
                      them.

MAXIM PADS -   Sold from a women's hygiene vending machine;
                      personal pads with the "Maxim" logo.

GULDEN'S NUGGETS -   Mustard flavored cheese snacks I would sell
                      out of the "Golden Nugget" Hotel.

ORE RIO'S -   Cookies with the "Rio" Hotel on them

HA HA CIENDAS -   Laughing ash trays. Pick it up, it laughs.

BAGELS & LUXOR -   Bagel sandwiches sold from my stand.

STARDUSTBUSTERS -   Dusters with "Stardust" across the feathers.

I would set up my stand by your gift shop or near your lobby. (Or
outside). We could work out the financial arrangements to your
liking. I'm thinking 50-50. That's usually fair for both
parties. The stand is very small compared to the massiveness of
your hotel. It would get lost in there; you wouldn't even notice
it. However, there are substantial profits to be made. I buy
hamburgers wholesale and can buy them cheaper than just one person
buying one hamburger. Let me know. The hamburger season is
coming upon us. (Sept 27th according to official weather
reports.). By Christmas we could have this thing humming. I'd
like to make this official. I'll start selling my Excaliburgers
and if anyone intervenes I'll show them this letter as I am
awaiting a reply from you. Thanks.

Respectfully,

Ted L. Nancy

EXCALIBUR

HOTEL / CASINO

August 29, 1995

Ted L. Nancy
560 North Moorpark Road, #236
Thousand Oaks, CA 91360

Dear Mr. Nancy:

Thank you for your letter regarding your products, in particular, the Excaliburger. It is, indeed, a "novel" idea.

As you may know, the hotel currently has several snack bars which handle a variety of fast food items, hamburgers included. Although your logo hamburger presents an interesting concept, it is not one that we are interested in pursuing at this time.

May you be successful in the sale of your other products.

Sincerely,

John F. Morocco
Food and Beverage Director

JFM/igs

cc: B. Prince

3850 Las Vegas Blvd. South, Las Vegas, Nevada 89109-4300 Mail: Post Office Box 96778, Las Vegas, Nevada 89193-6778
Telephone: (702) 597-7777 Toll-Free Reservations: (800) 937-7777
A CIRCUS CIRCUS ENTERPRISE

560 No. Moorpark Rd. #236
Thousand Oaks, CA 91360

JOHN F. MOROCCO
FOOD & BEVERAGE DIRECTOR
EXCALIBUR HOTEL & CASINO
P.O. Box 96778
Las Vegas, NV 89193-6778   Sept. 3, 1995

Dear Mr. Morocco,

Thank you for answering my letter regarding my "EXCALIBURGERS."
Those are the hamburgers that are shaped like the Excalibur
Hotel that I wanted to sell in your lobby.

I want to tell you how embarrassed I am, Sir, for wasting your
time with what I now consider to be a bad idea. In thinking
this idea over I now realize how poor of an idea it was. I
don't know what I was thinking. Hamburgers in the shape of your
hotel would not be popular. Most people would not want their
food in the same shape as where they are sleeping. I am deeply
embarrassed.

When I realized I was bothering the Food and Beverage Director I
thought I had done a pretty stupid thing. I had no idea this
letter would go to you. I thought it would go to the Front
Desk, concierge, maybe the coffee shop for approval. But I did
not think that you, Sir, would receive a letter which I now am
embarrassed of.

To sell hamburgers in the shape of the Excalibur Hotel & Casino
is a stupid idea. Nobody would eat them. Most people like
their hamburgers round, not in the shape of a castle. I am very
sorry that I have wasted your time with this hamburger idea. I
can honestly tell you that I will not bother you any more,
Excalibur. You are a favorite hotel of mine and I enjoy
visiting there. (And eating too!) I now realize my ideas for
hotel products is a foolish one. Although I do have interest
in the Maxim Pads, but not from the hotel. Those things would
sell!

Please accept this as my deepest apologies for wasting your time
with my previous letter. I am truly sorry.

With All The Respect I Have,

Ted L. Nancy

Ted L. Nancy

P.S. You have great Horseradish sauce!

EXCALIBUR
HOTEL / CASINO
3850 Las Vegas Blvd. South, Las Vegas, Nevada 89119-1050
Mail: Post Office Box 96778, Las Vegas, Nevada 89193-6778
Telephone: (702) 597-7777   Toll-Free Res: (800) 937-7777

Food and Beverage

Ted L. Nancy
560 North Moorpark Road, #236
Thousand Oaks, CA 91360

560 N. Moorpark Rd., #236
Thousand Oaks, CA 91360

EXECUTIVE OFFICES
HOLIDAY INN HOTELS
3796 Lamar
Memphis, TN 38195   Sept. 15, 1995

Dear Holiday Inn Hotels:

In this competitive world of competition we have to be one
better than our competitors. I think a wonderful Holiday Inn
Hotel promotion would be:

"Free Use Of The Housekeeping Cart." A person's stay includes
unlimited use of the maid's cart in the hallway. As many soaps
as you like, pens, shampoo. Just help yourself when you see the
cart in the hall.

I think that this idea would skyrocket. People I know all
complain that they never get enough of those little soaps and
shampoos in their rooms. Whenever the see the cart they hit it.
Those bath gels are great too! Where else can you get this
stuff?   Whenever I return from a trip I have plenty of those
little conditioners and lotions. That's when I think what a
great hotel!

If you advertised that a person could have free unlimited use of
the maid's housekeeping cart people would flock to your hotel.
What do you think?   I think Holiday Inns are the best to stay
at when traveling as a group.   Hoping to hear from you soon.
How can I find out if the Holiday Inn's have non smoking rooms?

Respectfully,

Ted L. Nancy

WORLDWIDE

Corporate Headquarters
Three Ravinia Drive
Suite 2000
Atlanta, GA 30346-2149
404-604-2000

October 19, 1995

Mr. Ted L. Nancy
560 N. Moorpark Road, #236
Thousand Oaks, California 91360

Dear Mr. Nancy:

Your letter of September 15th has finally made its way to our Corporate office of 5 years here in Atlanta!

We have considered your creative ideas and suggestions for the "Free Use of the Housekeeping Cart". The objective of making sure our customers get everything they need while staying at Holiday Inn hotels has merit. You can imagine that unlimited use of the housekeeping cart would cause quite a liability for the hotel operators and keeping the cart well-stocked would mean additional labor on hotel staff.

In order to assist our many franchisees with servicing guests while maintaining some control on their financial obligations we provide the "Forget Something" service as a rule of operation at all Holiday Inn hotels. Forget Something provides guests with many items they may need or forget while traveling -- shampoos, toothbrushes, comb, brush, and so on.

Please feel free to take advantage of this service on your travels to Holiday Inn hotels in the future. And, thank you for taking the time to put your comments in writing to us. We appreciate hearing from our guests first hand!

Sincerely,

Annette Cornely
Marketing Specialist

P.S. Non-smoking rooms are also available at all Holiday Inn hotels. You may request these when making your reservation by calling 1-800-HOLIDAY, although it cannot be guaranteed until time of check-in.

Holiday Inns, Inc., A Bass Company

Bass

560 No. Moorpark Rd. #236
Thousand Oaks, CA 91360

President
TOPPS BASEBALL CARD COMPANY
One Whitehall Street
New York, NY 10004   Jan 13, 1996

Dear Topps Baseball Card President:

I have a valuable which I would like to donate to the great Topps
card company because you stand for an American baseball
institution. As a boy, I flipped your cards for hours.

In 1960, I was an employee of a hotel in Miami Beach, Florida
where Mr. Mickey Mantle was staying. About two in the afternoon,
I was summoned to Mr. Mantle's room to deliver room service to
him. He ordered an egg salad sandwich and an ice tea. I'll never
forget it as long as I live.

As I was setting up the room service tray, I noticed Mr. Mantle
clipping his toenails. I watched out of the corner of my eye as
he clipped every toe. He had trouble with the last nail but
eventually his diligence paid off. At that moment, the telephone
rang and Mr. Mantle was called from his room. He told me to leave
the egg salad sandwich and he would eat it later. I'll never
forget his words for the rest of my life. He left the room. I
dropped to the carpet and secured all the toenails that had been
clipped off. There are almost ten toenails. Nine and some
shavings but a full set.

I would like to donate this collectible to your card company. You
have made children of all ages very happy. Perhaps this valuable
could even be put on a card. They collect everything else! I
think that Mr. Mantle was a great player. These toenails should
be enjoyed by his millions of fans. Any time you can see
something directly off a celebrity, that is better than any
picture or autograph. This is something truly from his body.

Please write me and tell me who I should send this gift to for
donation. Thank you.

Sincerely,

Ted L. Nancy

NATIONAL BASEBALL HALL OF FAME AND MUSEUM, INC.

March 12, 1996

Ted L. Nancy
560 No. Moorpark Road #236
Thousand Oaks, CA 91360

Dear Mr. Nancy:

Si Berger, of the Topps Baseball Card Company, forwarded your letter of January 13th to the Hall of Fame and my attention.

We are very interested in your story of the Mickey Mantle toenails, and how you obtained them in Miami Beach in 1960 while delivering room service.

This is a fascinating tale, and we would like to know more about the condition of the nails, and what shape they are in. We have an Accessions Committee which meets periodically to review potential donations to the Hall, and we would be most interested in knowing more about the toenails, and why you wish to offer them to the museum.

If it is possible to send us a picture or the nails, we would be interested in examining them before we reach any decision.

Thank you for thinking of the historical importance of these items, and attempting to place them in an institution where they will be saved for future generations to enjoy.

Sincerely,

Peter P. Clark
Registrar

560 N. Moorpark Rd., #236
Thousand Oaks, CA. 91360

Jul 11, 1995

President,
MARS CANDY COMPANY
High Street
Hackettstown, NJ 07840

Dear Mars Candy Pesident,

I have been eating candy my entire life. People in my
neighborhood say I can tell what kind of candy is in my mouth
with my eyes blindfolded.

 My favorites are Snickers. It seems you mix a lot of things
togeher to get your candy. Nuts, caramel, chocolate.

My question: How can you add peanut butter to a Snickers and
call it a Peanut Butter Snickers? It's no longer a Snickers.
The peanut butter is a brand new candy and should get its own
name.

Also, how about this for a new candy bar - picture a
Butterfinger - only instead of peanut butter the center is
banana. Crunchy banana. With the texture and consistency
similar to a Butterfingers inside. You could call it a
"Nanacrumble."

Also, the name Snickers is bad. Sounds like somebody is
laughing at you. Can it be changed? How 'bout "Snuuckers."
Make it sound like the Hagen Dazs people with a foreign name.

Thanks for years and years of chocolate heaven. (I gave up on
the skin a long time ago).

Is there any way to get information about what new candy bars
you are planning to introduce? Thanks for taking the time to
read my letter. I hope I hear from you.

Chocolate! It's our best snack!

Ted L. Nancy

a division of Mars, Incorporated

High Street, Hackettstown, New Jersey 07840 ● Telephone 908-852-1000

July 21, 1995

Mr. Ted L. Nancy
#236
560 N. Moorpark Road
Thousand Oaks, CA 91360

Dear Mr. Nancy:

It was very thoughtful of you to take the time to offer your ideas
regarding SNICKERS® Bar. At M&M/MARS, we have an extensive Research
and Development staff whose sole responsibility is to design, develop
and refine product ideas. Sometimes this process can take years before
a finished product can be marketed. To avoid confusion of ownership, we
must refuse the thousands of suggestions we receive every year.
Although we appreciate your interest, we hope you will understand our
business position.

Thank you again for writing. We appreciate hearing from our fine
consumers. Please accept the enclosed complimentary store coupon for
your continued enjoyment of M&M/MARS products.

Sincerely,

Adella Kowalski
Consumer Affairs

AMK/bww 0444728A
Enclosure

560 N. Moorpark Rd., #236
Thousand Oaks, CA. 91360

MS. ADELLA KOWALSKI
MARS CANDY COMPANY
High Street
Hackettstown, NJ 07840   Aug 9, 1995

Dear Ms. Kowalski,

Thank you very, very much for the candy certificates. What a
nice gesture. I immediately went out and redeemed one for some
SKITTLES and bought some STARBURST on my own. During an
involuntary experimentation, I placed a STARBURST and a SKITTLES
into my mouth at the same time and WOW! I was STARTLED. There's
a new candy right there -- STARTLES. "Hey, everyone's getting
STARTLED! STARTLES - by MARS.

According to your letter, you have people there that spend
"years" making up this stuff. I came up with this in a day.
Here's some other one's I thought of that day:

CHEWYBALLS - Marshmallow covered in caramel. Watch out on hot
days. It's almost a drink!

TA TA BAR - Baby's first candy bar. Vitamin fortified.

SINGLES BAR - Eat when you're available. With or without nuts.

Hey, one of them is good. You figure. Years of research?
Hah! I thought of this in the morning. How about this: You
make it -- if no one buys it, you stop making it. It costs the
same and takes less time. I can do this stuff daily. Any job
openings? Also, the name "SKITTLES." Can it be changed?
Sounds like an old Navy drinking disease. Men in WW2 used to
come home with a case of the skittles. It was a mess!

Thank you very, very much for listening to my ideas, Ma'am. I
know you are very, very busy there but it's nice to know that a
company as busy as yours STOPS to listen to its customers. I
Also think of potato chip names if it ever comes up. I look
forward to your reply. The best BARS are from MARS! Also, are
you related to the wrestler? I saw him grapple many, many
times. VERY GOOD! If you are related than say hello to my
favorite wrestler for me. He was the best at the cartwheel
roll! Hey, there's a candy! The Cartwheel Roll. Thanks very
much!

Ted L. Nancy
"...the Kirk Gibson of candy makers..."
SWEETS, SNACKS, AND STUFF - Feb '95 issue

STILL WAITING FOR REPLY!

m&m·MARS

a division of Mars, Incorporated
High Street
Hackettstown, New Jersey 07640

Recycle

HACKETTSTOWN
N.J.
JUL 21 '95
6105031

U.S.POSTAGE
= 0.32

MR TED L NANCY
#236
560 N MOORPARK ROAD
THOUSAND OAKS CA 91360

AMK

Ted L. Nancy
560 N. Moorpark Rd. #236
Thousand Oaks, CA 91360

HANES UNDERWEAR
P.O. Box 3013
Winston Salem, N.C.
27102   Aug 23, 1995

Dear Underwear Executives:

I have been an avid Hanes underwear wearer for years, except for a
brief period in '88 when I tried Jockey Shorts.

I have examined my underpants for many years. Always I wondered
why nothing dramatic has happened in men's underpants wear for
such a long time. That need not be anymore.

Hanes, I am pleased to announce that I have invented the "SIX DAY
UNDERWEAR." It has three leg hole openings. Every other day, you
rotate and move over one leg hole opening. At the end of three
days they've become completely reversible and you begin again –
thus your SIX DAY UNDERWEAR.

A cleaning agent in the fabric launders the shorts, agitating as
you move about, then dispenses the lint onto your legs. When the
briefs are washed, enzyme adhesives in the fabric attach
themselves to just enough detergent (anionic surfactants) to last
another week.

If there is any interest, I would appreciate meeting with the
proper executive(s).

I am the creator of the 'NaNa Krumble' and the 'TaTa Bar.'

I look forward to hearing from you.

Sincerely,

Ted L. Nancy
Ted L. Nancy
Inventor

P.O. Box 2760
Winston-Salem North Carolina 27102

470 Hanes Mill Road
Winston-Salem, North Carolina 27105

Telephone: (910) 519-2011
General Telex: 62940931
Trademark Telex: 62840635
Telecopier: (910) 519-7312

September 20, 1995

Writer's Direct Dial Number:

Mr. Ted Nancy
560 N. Moorpark Rd. #236
Thousand Oaks, California 91360

Dear Mr. Nancy:

Your letter regarding your product idea has been referred to me for response.

The legal implications of receiving offers, suggestions, or ideas from outside our company are such that we have a policy which requires the execution of our standard idea submission agreement before we convey to the submitter our evaluation of the idea. This agreement is for the benefit of the submitter as well. Two copies of this are enclosed for your review.

We do feel that you should be aware that Sara Lee maintains a staff of creative marketing personnel and product development personnel whose primary responsibilities lie in the areas of creating new marketing concepts and products. To some extent, use is also made of outside advertising and public relations agencies. For these reasons, Sara Lee has had under consideration at some point in the past numerous ideas and concepts and even now may be testing or evaluating such ideas.

If you find the terms of the agreement acceptable, please sign and date both copies, and return one to me, retaining the other copy for your records. When the agreement is received, your submitted materials will be reviewed by the appropriate personnel in our company who can determine if there is any present interest. Upon completion of this review, we will contact you.

Thank you for your inquiry and interest. I look forward to hearing from you soon.

Very truly yours,

Ann B. Johnson

Ann B. Johnson

/aj
Enclosures

LA$ VEGAS HERE I COME

I'm Gonna Party 'Til My Pants Fall Down!!!

560 North Moorpark Road
TownHome #236
Thousand Oaks, California 91360

Reservation Desk
FLAMINGO HILTON HOTEL & CASINO
3555 Las Vegas Blvd South
Las Vegas, NV 89109   January 12, 1996

Dear Flamingo Hotel Reservations,

I am interested in checking in to your hotel the week of February
26th. I have heard that your hotel is very hospitable to its
guests; especially gamblers and card players. I am both! I have
a situation which I would like to address prior to my visit. I
have lucky clothes which I like to gamble in.

I will be dressed as a shrimp. That is a reddish veiny body
outfit with a brittle curved fantail. The top of my head will be
hardish and crunchy and have tarter sauce on it. (Not real!)
I will wear orangish foam shoes that match the rest of the outfit.
This is my lucky clothing that I have gambled in before. (Mostly
European cruises). I feel comfortable in this outfit and relaxed.

I know Flamingo goes out of its way to please their gamblers.
Even if they are in shrimp clothing.

Please let me know if the February 26th date is ok for me to check
in, then come down to the casino and gamble dressed as a shrimp?
Thanks. I am making my travel plans now, so I must know if the
week of the 26th is confirmed. It is my vacation time. I need to
relax. Thank you very much for getting back to me on this.

Sincerely,

Ted L. Nancy

Ted L. Nancy

HILTON
LAS VEGAS

January 24, 1996

Ted L. Nancy
560 North Moorpark Road
Townhome #236
Thousand Oaks, CA 91360

Dear Mr. Nancy:

Thank you very much for your letter of January 12, expressing an
interest in staying with us at the Flamingo Hilton in Las Vegas.

It is our goal, as you state in your letter, to be hospitable to
our guests and make their visit one that they will remember. It is
very important to us that our guests feel comfortable and relaxed
during their stay; however, regarding your request to gamble in
shrimp attire, we feel that because of the high level of activity
created by the outfit, it might be too distractive.

If you feel that you would like to visit us and would be able to
relax and gamble in street attire, we would be very happy to host
you on your upcoming vacation.

Again, Mr. Nancy, thank you very much for your correspondence, it
was a pleasure to hear from you.

Sincerely,

FLAMINGO HILTON LAS VEGAS

Christopher Abraham
Director of Casino Marketing

CA/kv

560 No. Moorpark Rd., #236
Thousand Oaks, CA. 91360

July 31, 1995

RESERVATIONS MANAGER
SAHARA HOTEL & CASINO
2535 Las Vegas Blvd So.
Las Vegas, NV 89109

Dear Sir Or Madam:

I am planning a Las Vegas excursion for the week of Sept 27th.
This week can be moved, but this is the best date. (Ink Spot Fest,
Coasters Grandma birthday, Cinnamon, etc.)

My question: I have my own drapes which I travel with. They are
special drapes (Made in Austria - not a knit) and help me keep
noise and light out. I will need NO HELP in putting these drapes
up. I have taken them down and put them up MANY times. I WILL
MAKE LITTLE MESS when I'm finished. All debris will be removed:
pins, hooks, string, etc.

I have always admired the Sahara for it's sheer ambience. I have
always liked the theme of the SAHARA. It's what Las Vegas is
about! The desert theme. Many times I have walked through your
beautiful hotel and have marveled at the sheer mass of it. And
now it is my time to stay at this magnificent hotel. The drapes
have been with me at other hotels. They are a lightweight fabric
(European) and wrinkle slightly. There is a stain in the left
hand corner (cat accident). I just didn't want HOUSEKEEPING to
wonder what these different drapes were. Didn't want anyone to be
startled.

So...please let me know If I can bring my own drapes to the Sahara
Hotel the week of Sept. 27th. (Or another week if that date is
busy).

Thank you very much, Sahara, for getting back to me on this. I
love your driveway.

Sincerely,

Ted L. Nancy
Travel Committee

SAHARA

HOTEL & CASINO

POST OFFICE BOX 98503 LAS VEGAS, NEVADA 89193
(702) 737-2111

August 9, 1995

Mr. Ted L. Nancy
560 North Moorpark Rd., #236
Thousand Oaks, CA   91360

Dear Mr. Nancy:

This is in response to your letter dated July 31, 1995,
in which you requested approval to bring your own drapes
with you.

Thank you for your complimentary remarks regarding the
Sahara. Unfortunately, I must respectfully deny your
request.

Sincerely,

SAHARA HOTEL AND CASINO

Susan K. Schulz
Hotel Manager

SKS:bc

560 No. Moorpark Rd., #236
Thousand Oaks, CA. 91360

Jan 3, 1996

Reservations Desk
SAHARA HOTEL & CASINO
2535 Las Vegas Blvd So.
Las Vegas, NV 89109

Dear Sahara Hotel:

I will be traveling to Las Vegas soon and very much want to
overnight stay at your fine hotel. I have seen pictures of it in
windows.

I travel with my own mirror. It is a full length mirror that I
keep with me always. It really does make me look the best. Other
mirrors make me look puffy, which I am not!

Although it is a large mirror and breakable (8' by 3') I maneuver
it around by myself. I will use the side stairwell when bringing
my mirror into your hotel. I wanted to alert you so that when I'm
out of the room during the day, my mirror is not accidentally
removed by your housekeepers. I can not use other mirrors as they
really don't make me look as good. (I am not chunky). I really
like the way I look in this mirror.

Please let me know if you have rooms available for the week of
March 8th. I'd like to check in with my mirror. Thanks. I love
your tile.

Sincerely,

Ted L. Nancy

Ted L. Nancy

SAHARA

HOTEL & CASINO

POST OFFICE BOX 98503 LAS VEGAS, NEVADA 89193
(702) 737-2111

JANUARY 16, 1996

TED L NANCY
560 NO. MOORPARK RD # 236
THOUSAND OAKS, CA 91360

DEAR MR. NANCY:

Thank you for your interest in the Sahara Hotel. We think you will
find the enclosed information useful. We offer a range of rates,
and will be happy to assist you in confirming your preference when
you place your reservation.

We request that you call to make reservations that include either
weekends or holidays as soon as you have definite plans. Periods
covering weekdays only should be made at least three weeks in
advance. One night's deposit is required on all reservations at
least fourteen days prior to arrival. To insure your dates, please
make sure the arrival date and the name of the guest appears on
the check.

Show reservations for our Congo Showroom may be made on the day of
the performance with the ticket booth. Show reservations for other
hotels may be made at our show ticket booth.

Cordially,

THE SAHARA HOTEL

Room Reservations

800-634-6666
VB/jh

560 No. Moorpark Rd #236
Thousand Oaks, CA 91360

January 12, 1996

General Manager
DEBBIE REYNOLDS HOTEL & CASINO
305 Convention Center Drive
Las Vegas, NV 89109

Dear General Manager:

I am interested in staying at your hotel for one week starting
February 21, 1996. I am part of a touring dinner theater group.
I have a dilemma.

I look exactly like Abraham Lincoln. How can I be safeguarded so
that others don't come up to me and pester me for autographs and
pictures with them? It can be very annoying in restaurants to sit
there looking like Abraham Lincoln and have people come up to you
and say they want to take a picture with you to show their kids.
I have tried to alter my appearance - I've had the mole removed -
but it is still a nuisance. I have dyed my hair and beard red but
to no avail. I have even taken the hat off. I still am bothered.
People love Lincoln! One guy tried to give me his Lincoln car
once, that's how impressed he was. I did not take it, of course.
But I have been in the tunnel.

Can an area in the coffee shop be sectioned off when I take my
meals? I do not drink liquids at dinner, so I am quick. Can the
proper hotel staff be notified that Abraham Lincoln's double is
eating and does not want to be pestered? This would be for the
entire week starting February 21st. Thank you for letting me know
regarding this situation, as I have to make my travel plans soon.
I have long admired the Debbie Reynolds Hotel for its family
atmosphere, good taste, and cornbread. That is why I chose to
stay here while others are staying elsewhere. Your hotel stands
for the clean Americana that this world needs. Even the lobby!
Having 'Abraham Lincoln' in your hotel, he would probably not be
as noticed as in other hotels. But I want to make sure. Thanks
for getting back to me on this. Are there rooms available on the
21st?

Sincerely,

Ted L. Nancy

HOTEL / CASINO / HOLLYWOOD MOVIE MUSEUM

January 17, 1996

Mr. Ted L. Nancy
560 No. Moorpark Road #236
Thousand Oaks, CA 91360

Dear Mr. Nancy:

Your letter of January 12 has been forwarded to me, and I do
empathize with your dilemma. I am sure that your appearance at
this resort will be treated with the same respect that has been
given to many of our celebrity guests, i.e. Rip Taylor, June
Allyson, Ann Miller, Donald O'Conner, Robert Wagner, Stephanie
Powers, Jane Powell - to name a few. Additionally, when not in
Hollywood making a movie, Debbie Reynolds frequents the hotel on a
daily basis; consequently, our staff has been exposed to quite a
distinctive guest list.

Thank you for including the Debbie Reynolds Hotel & Casino in your
travel plans in February; and at the present time, accommodations
are available during the dates you mentioned. The prevailing rate
for February 21st and 22nd is $79.00 and the 23rd through the 27th
is $89.00.   Please call Toll Free 800 633-1777 and our Room
Reservation Department will gladly take your reservation.

Looking forward to your visit with us.

Sincerely,

Henry Ricci
Chief of Operations

560 No. Moorpark Rd. #236
Thousand Oaks, CA 91360

MR. HENRY RICCI
Chief Of Operations
DEBBIE REYNOLDS HOTEL & CASINO
305 Convention Center Drive
Las Vegas, NV 89109   January 29, 1996

Dear Mr. Ricci,

Thank you for your response to my letter regarding my future visit
to the Debbie Reynolds Hotel and Casino in Las Vegas and the fact
that I look like Abraham Lincoln.

But, Sir, with all due respect, I cannot be compared to Rip
Taylor. I am the 16th President Of The United States. He throws
confetti. I am a log splitter, a not so easy accomplishment.
While I have enjoyed Rip Taylor over the years, and I think he is
a terrific entertainer, and I have even been sprinkled by his
confetti, I am the President Of The United States. Abraham
Lincoln was a great statesman. He had the dignity and respect of
many. When he walked into a room, you knew you were with a
leader. A person that cared for all. People treat me like
Abraham Lincoln. They call me Abe or Mr. Lincoln or Mr.
President. My name is Ted. So if people treat me like the
President, I suppose I should be accorded the due respect. As a
result...

Can I be ASSURED that I will have privacy at your hotel? Can I
get a security guard to walk me to the restaurant when I take my
meals? We don't need another incident! I need to know that I can
have 'a little extra' when it comes to my safety. (Along with the
shampoos, soaps, wash cloths, sewing kit).

Please get back to me on this. The February 21st start date is
coming up fast. (Lincoln's birthday). I appreciate your response
so I can make my reservations now. Also, can I take my meals in
my room? Do you offer that service? And can ONLY the hotel
staff know of my route through the hotel? Thank you very much,
Mr. Ricci. Debbie Reynolds should know what a dedicated employee
she has. It is nice that you care about your guests and that you
try and accommodate them. That's important in this world. People
like you make traveling easier. I will always stay at the Debbie
Reynolds Hotel if I can be accomodated. Do you have a
presidential suite?
Sincerely,

Ted L. Nancy
Ted L. Nancy

HOTEL / CASINO / HOLLYWOOD MOVIE MUSEUM

February 2, 1996

Mr. Ted L. Nancy
560 No. Moorpark Road #236
Thousand Oaks, CA 91360

Dear Mr. Nancy:

In response to your most recent letter; currently, we are sold out on February 22, 23 and 24.

For your information, we do not have a Presidential Suite at this facility nor do we have a Security Officer to assign to any one guest. However, Room Service is available from 6:00 AM to 10:00 PM daily.

Sorry we cannot accommodate you this time, but there is always the possibility something may open up closer to those dates if you should care to check with our Room Reservations Department (800) 633-1777.

Thank you for your interest in the Debbie Reynolds Hotel & Casino.

Sincerely,

Henry Bicci
Chief of Operations

305 Convention Center Dr. Las Vegas, NV 89109
702 734-0711 FAX 702 734-2954 RESERVATIONS 800 633-1777

560 No. Moorpark Rd. #236
Thousand Oaks, CA 91360

August 5, 1996

Slots Department Manager
HACIENDA HOTEL & CASINO
3950 Las Vegas Blvd South
Las Vegas, NV 89109

Dear Slots Manager:

I understand the Hacienda Hotel will be holding an all nude slot
tournament. When? Can I get ALL information regarding this
event? Also, do you have any other nude gaming events? I love
gambling naked. It's really the only way to insure against
cheating.

Will a portion of your casino be isolated off for this totally
nude gambling experience? There will be plenty of us. I can
organize over 120 unclothed gamblers from our club. Slots, poker,
pai-gow, roulette, craps. We want to gamble at all these naked.

Our nudists have enjoyed nude gambling all over Europe without
incident excluding a misinterpreted gesture in France.

In your nude slot tournament is the dealer also naked? They would
not have to be totally nude. A dealers apron would be fine.
Also, what will the prizes be? In the Europe gambling event
everyone got one free lucky pull. (I won)!

Please let me know when this nude slot tournament is. And can the
hotel give us a package rate for our nude club of approximately
120 naked gamblers?

I look forward to hearing from you soon. Thank you.

Sincerely,

Ted L. Nancy

HACIENDA
HOTEL · CASINO · LAS VEGAS

August 16, 1996

Ted L. Nancy
560 No. Moorpark Rd. #236
Thousand Oaks, CA 91360

Dear Mr. Nancy:

Thank you for your recent inquiry regarding an all nude slot tournament. I regret
to inform you that the Hacienda Hotel & Casino does not hold such an event.

However, should we decide to schedule one, we will be sure to let you know in
advance.

Sincerely,

Bill Boswell
Slot Director

3950 Las Vegas Boulevard South · Las Vegas, Nevada 89119 · 702-739-8911

560 N. Moorpark Rd. #236
Thousand Oaks, Ca 91360

30 Jul 95

RESERVATIONS MANAGER
GOLDEN NUGGET HOTEL & CASINO
129 Fremont St.
Las Vegas, NV 89101

Dear Hotel Reservations Mgr:

I am planning a Western drive through excursion in an older car
and will be arriving: Las Vegas, Nevada on Sept 27, 1995. I will
have been on the road then five (5) days with minimal sleep. The
car is a 61 year old Buick.

I was wondering if I could bring my own MATTRESS into my room and
sleep on that? I will need NO HELP in bringing this mattress into
the hotel. I travel with this mattress and sleep on it. I get my
best sleep on this mattress and it has been recommended to me that
I sleep on this mattress every chance I get. It really does work!

I will take the mattress up the side stairwell so as to avoid any
confusion with the gamblers at the tables. I can weave this
mattress through the side of the casino avoiding MOST of the
gaming tables. Then I will be down there myself gambling
(EVERYTHING: CRAPS. POKER, SLOTS!!!) as soon as I set this thing
set up. (Sheets, pad, vents, etc.).

Let me know If I can bring my own mattress into the GOLDEN NUGGET
beginning Sept. 27th. I can postpone drive time to accommodate
the Hotel's room scheduling. In other words, this would be my
best time to arrive but I'm not married to it. Thank you for
letting me know about this. I need to know! This mattress is
important to me and so is the Golden Nugget. I am a long time
gambler there! I would like to stay with my own mattress!!

Sincerely,

Ted L. Nancy
Ted L. Nancy

GOLDEN NUGGET

August 30, 1995

Mr. Ted L. Nancy
560 N. Moorpark Road #236
Thousand Oaks, Ca 91360

Dear Mr. Nancy:

I am in receipt of your letter dated July 30, 1995, and apologize for the delay in responding to you in writing.

I would like to respond to your inquiry about bringing your own mattress into the Golden Nugget. We have recently replaced the mattresses in all of our guestrooms. We also have bed boards or mattress toppers that may be requested from our Housekeeping Department at no charge that would make your stay more comfortable.

It is our hotel policy that no furniture of any type be removed from or rearranged in a guestroom. We certainly hope you understand this policy. We look forward to the opportunity to welcome you to the Golden Nugget. If you have any further questions, please do not hesitate to contact my office.

Sincerely,

Franz Kallao

Franz Kallao
Front Office Manager

FK/em

 POST OFFICE BOX 610, LAS VEGAS, NEVADA 89125, (702) 385-7111

560 No. Moorpark Rd.
Apt #236
Thousand Oaks, CA   91360

Aug 6, 1996

Showroom Tickets
LAS VEGAS HILTON HOTEL & CASINO
3000 Paradise Rd.
Las Vegas, Nevada 89109

Dear Ticket Personnel:

I have been saving to see Elvis Presley in concert at the Las
Vegas Hilton for a long time. Soon I will get my chance! I want
to make reservations for his Sept 11, 1996 show. Can I get a good
seat? How much is it? I need one.

I have always admired Mr. Presley's singing even though he is
heavier today. Will he be singing his earlier favorites "Hound
Dog" and the suede shoe song?   I like those.

I have seen pictures of your wonderful hotel and the encased Elvis
suit. I'm going to swim in your pool too. How much are golf and
crap lessons?

I also understand it will be very hot in Las Vegas during that
time. I hope this will be an indoor concert as I am allowed only
2 hours in scorching heat before I blister. I have a condition
where I must wear a safety pad.

Please send me info: Hotel room rate for one night, Sept 11,
1996. I may need an extra ottoman for my oversized feet. And
ticket price for Elvis Presley in concert the same night. (A good
seat, please). I want to finally see this show! Thank you.

Sincerely,

Ted L. Nancy

Ted L. Nancy

Las Vegas Hilton

August 12, 1996

Ted L. Nancy
560 No. Moorpark Rd.
Apt. #236
Thousand Oaks, CA 91360

Dear Mr. Nancy:

Thank you for your letter expressing interest in entertainment at
the Las Vegas Hilton.

On September 11, Andrew Lloyd Webber's "Starlight Express" will be
featured in the Starlight Theatre (which is indoors) at 7:30 p.m.
Starlight Express opened at the Las Vegas Hilton on September 23,
1993 and has been rolling along ever since. This powerful Broadway
musical was voted the #1 show in Las Vegas by the Las Vegas Review
Journal Reader's Poll for 1995.

We have enclosed a leaflet with show times and prices. We look
forward to hearing from you in the near future.

Thank you,

The Ticket Office

enclosure

560 No. Moorpark Rd #236
Thousand Oaks, CA 91360

1/3/96

Reservations
PALACE STATION HOTEL & CASINO
P.O. Box 26448
Las Vegas, NV 89126-0448

Dear Palace Station:

I want to check into your hotel on Jan 31, 1996. I travel with my
own soda pop vending machine. I find this soda machine to be far
superior to any soda machines in any hotel I have ever stayed in.
It is good for my thirst and I carry most flavors. (Yours does
not have orange!)

Is this a problem, checking in with it and bringing it into my
room? I can lift it myself even though it is a standard size soft
drink vending machine. This soda machine is important to me, both
for physical comfort and also for mental relaxation. It will stay
in my room for my thirst only. Then I won't have to go into the
hallway with a bunch of quarters. I am not selling soda.

So...please let me know of I can check in with my own soda machine
the night of January 31st? Thanks, Palace Station, I have heard
that you are exceptionally nice to your guests and go out of your
way to accommodate them when it comes to their own vending
machines. That is why I will ALWAYS stay at the Palace Station
Hotel. And I will always return my room key promptly.

Sincerely,

Ted L. Nancy
Ted L. Nancy

January 9, 1996

Mr Ted l Nancy
560 N Moorpark Rd. #236
Thousand Oaks, Ca. 91360

Dear Mr. Nancy:

Thank you for your inquiry regarding your soda vending machine. At this time we are
unable to accommodate your request.

We would like to let you know that we will stock whatever flavor of soda you desire in
Room Service for you. Please call us a few days before you arrive and we will be
glad to to stock any flavor of your choice.

Please do not hesitate to call us at 800-634-3101.

Sincerely,

The Station Casinos Reservations Team

560 N. Moorpark Rd. #236
Thousand Oaks, CA. 91360

RESERVATIONS
CIRCUS CIRCUS
2880 Las Vegas Blvd. South
Las Vegas, Nevada 89109   Jul 15, 1995

Dear Sir Or Madam:

I would like to stay at your hotel and would like to know if
it's possible if I bring my own chair? I would be staying for
one week (Week of Sept 27th preferably) and have a special vinyl
easy chair that I like to relax on.

I would need minimal help in getting in and out of the hotel.
(I can carry it myself most places). However, I would probably
need to take the room door off at the hinges (I have had to do
this many times).

I will make little commotion in the lobby as I can bring this
chair up the side stairwell. I may need a bellman to help with
the cushions.

Plese let me know if bringing my own chair into your hotel would
be ok for the duration of my Guest stay. Thank you. Circus
Circus is the best!

Sincerely,

Ted L. Nancy

HOTEL • CASINO/LAS VEGAS, NEVADA

July 27, 1995

Mr. Ted L. Nancy
560 N. Moorpark Road #236
Thousand Oaks CA 91360

Dear Mr. Nancy:

I am writing in response to your letter concerning a future visit.

That would be acceptable to bring your own chair during your visit in September.

Sincerely,

Jim Friesen
Hotel Manager
CIRCUS CIRCUS HOTEL/CASINO

JF:nb

LOOKIN' FOR WORK

My resume speaks for itself

Ted L. Nancy
560 No. Moorpark Rd. #236
Thousand Oaks, CA 91360

General Manager
RINGLING BROTHERS CIRCUS
267 South Tamiami Trail
Nokomis, Fla.
34275   Nov 25, 1995

Hello Ringling Circus,

I am 2 foot 3 inches tall, weigh 65 pounds, and perform as PIP THE
MIGHTY SQUEAK. I will perform in your circus for up to 3 hours
balancing things on me, dancing, mimicking, and generally being
entertaining. I do a self contained act where I stand in one
small area and sing, dance, skate around, twirl, balance, tumble,
stop and start, run in different directions in various speeds
coming to abrupt, extended, sliding stops, generally entertain.
The show is 2 hours and 25 minutes long. I can lift 80 pounds
bent over.

I lift a 100 pound woman on my back. (From audience). I shuffle
cards, dance, I tell stories, I balance an orange on my forehead
and move about for 2 hours and 25 minutes. I can break this up
into 3 minute increments for smaller circumstances. Or I can do
two 1 hour and 10 minute shows. But with the longer show you get
5 more minutes. The kids love me!

I charge $550.00 which includes my 20 costume changes. I bring a
little screen to change behind, then come out and perform again.
Nobody can see me change behind the screen if it is situated
right. People love me!

I wish to perform in The Ringling Brothers Circus. I admire your
circus for a long time and now wish to be in it. Audiences have
flocked throughout Europe and the Bahamas, Canada and Tonga to see
my specialty show. I am truly entertaining. I stretch, shout,
flex, call out names, lift a man from the audience and move in a
circle with him. I hum. I bark.

Please let me know who I apply to at Ringling Brothers to join
your circus? Send me the forms and direct me to the proper
personnel. Thank you. I can be reached at 560 No. Moorpark Rd.
#236, Thousand Oaks, CA 91360. Thanks!

Sincerely,

Ted L. Nancy
Pip The Mighty Squeak

February 23, 1996

Mr. Ted L. Nancy
560 No. Moorpark Rd. #236
Thousand Oaks, CA 91360

Dear Mr. Nancy,

Thank you for your interest in performing with "The Greatest Show On Earth". We appreciate your interest and are always looking for new talent. We ask you to send a video of your performance that we can review. If you would please send this video as soon as possible as we are preparing for next years show.

Thank you for thinking of Ringling Bros. and Barnum & Bailey .

Sincerely,

Jim Ragona
Talent & Production Coordinator

560 No. Moorpark Rd. #236
Thousand Oaks, CA 91360

Mr. Paul J. Orfalea
Chairperson Of The Board
KINKO'S COPIES
P.O. Box 8000
Ventura, Ca 93002-9928   12/11/95

Dear Mr. Orfalea,

As the Chairperson of the Board Of Kinkos Copy Centers I thought I
would approach you with this suggestion. I am a Siamese Twin. My
name is Ted, my brother's name is Lyle. We are connected at the
shoulders. We do not face each other, so we both can do TWO
DIFFERENT jobs at the SAME TIME. We would like to work in a
Kinkos.

This is the type of work both myself and Lyle can easily do. I can
copy while he rings up a customer. I think a Siamese Twin working
at your * Kinkos would be terrific publicity. Copies by a twin.
Maybe that could be your advertising. Talk about the ultimate
copy!

Anyway, what do you say? We are good workers and just want the
chance to blend in. We are not looking for any special favors.
Just a chance to show that we can be valuable employees. I
thought I would write to you since you are certainly in a high
enough position that you could hire us.

Believe me it is tough being a Siamese Twin but we try and get
along the best way. It's VERY hard to find employment. Most
people gawk at us. Luckily only one of us can see that. Is there
any job openings for a qualified employee(s)? We are for real and
very anxious to blend in.   Thanks.

Respectfully,

Ted L. Nancy

December 14, 1995

Mr. Ted L. Nancy
560 N. Moorpark Road, #236
Thousand Oaks, CA 91360

Dear Mr. Nancy:

Thank you for your letter expressing an interest in employment opportunities with Kinko's.

I have forwarded your correspondence to Mary Jane McCracken, Kinko's Human Resources Manager. Please contact Mary Jane directly at 652-4135 regarding opportunities at Kinko's that would fit the qualifications of you and your brother.

Again, thank you. Your interest in Kinko's as a potential employer is appreciated.

Sincerely,

Paul J. Orfalea
Chairperson of the Board

c: Mary Jane McCracken, Human Resources Manager, HR&D, Kinko's, Inc.

560 No. Moorpark Rd. #236
Thousand Oaks, CA 91360

MS. Mary Jane McCracken
Human Resources Manager
KINKOS COPIES
255 West Stanley Ave
Ventura, CA 93002

Jan 24, 1996

Dear MS. McCracken,

I would like to thank Kinkos so much for having the Chairperson of
Kinkos address my special needs. I (we) would like to come in for
an interview except there is one problem for now. My Siamese twin
brother, Lyle, hurt his back playing basketball. He's all laid
out. He won't be on his feet for another 4 weeks. So to come in
myself while he is groggy from medication won't make much sense.
Would it? He is an avid sportsman while I like to play my
trombone. Also, he may be going on vacation.

I really appreciate the opportunity to work at Kinkos. I can sort
incoming faxes while Lyle helps a customer. Lyle can staple and
collate, while I stamp hands. We really can do 2 jobs for the
same price as 1 1/2 people. (That's what we tell people. We are a
lot of fun. We try and keep a good sense of humor). We wear 1
shirt. So...when Lyle is better can we come in for an
appointment? When will be the best time?

Please let me know what date in February (after the 24th) we could
see you for an appointment. I want you to meet both of us and see
what good workers I (we) are am. Thank you very much for reaching
out to 2 people that really can get along as 2 people. I'll bet
you 2 regular people argue more than us. Thank you very much.

Respectfully,

Ted L. Nancy
Ted L. Nancy
Lyle

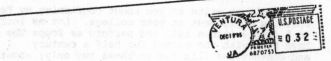

560 No. Moorpark Rd. #236
Thousand Oaks, CA 91360

Public Relations
UNIVERSITY OF TEXAS SAN ANTONIO
6900 North Loop
1604 West
San Antonio, TX 78249   Jan 13, 1996

Dear University Of Texas,

I was told to write to you about confirming my Feb 21, 1996
speaking engagement at your college. Let me introduce myself. I
am 8 feet 3 inches tall and perform as Topps The Slender Giant. I
have been with the circus for half a century. I talk at schools
and conventions (limited to these two only) about my circus
experiences. (Will not talk about kitchen incident). I performed
for over eight years as Topps the Shoeless Giant. Two years as
Topps The Heavy Giant. One year as Topps the Stumbling Giant. I
will talk about that. I was with European, Bahamian, and Canadian
circuses. I have performed before the King Of Tonga, His Majesty
King Taufa'Ahau Tupou IV. And I have Palace stationary. We
thought we had shared a same address. Some people call me a Lou
Rawls look alike.

I speak against the perils of bad living; Navy living. Cigar shop
living. I am open about all my experiences. I hold nothing back.
In this talk you hear a frank and candid account of the circus and
carnival life, as sick as it is. I think I am an education for
students and teachers, and all alike. It is a 90 minute talk
followed by questions on what it was like to be a circus
performer, a giant, very thin, very heavy, a marijuana addict,
conjugal visits, an alcoholic (Schnapps), and a telemarketer. The
talk is very entertaining, sprinkled with colorful recollections.
There are no expletives! I do make one (1) foul gesture, but
only as part of a story.

Please write and let me know if the Feb 21 date is confirmed, as I
was told. I also need to know about publicity. Thank you very
much. My mailing address is 560 No. Moorpark Rd. #236 Thousand
Oaks, CA 91360.

Respectfully,

Ted Nancy

Ted L. Nancy
Topps The Slender Giant

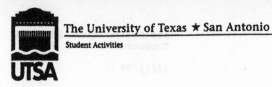

The University of Texas ★ San Antonio

Student Activities

UTSA

January 22, 1996

Ted L. Nancy
560 No. Moorpark Rd. #236
Thousand Oaks, CA 91360

Dear Mr. Nancy;

I am writing in response to the letter I received from you on January 19, 1996, which requested confirmation for a performance by Tops The Slender Giant on the UTSA campus on February 21, 1996. The Student Activities Office of UTSA never contracted for this program, and does not confirm the engagement at our University.

If you have any further questions, please feel free to contact me at (210) 691-4160.

Thank you,

Brenda Bellamy
Program Coordinator

560 No. Moorpark Rd. #236
Thousand Oaks, CA 91360

12/14/95

Promotions Office
MINNESOTA TWINS
501 Chicago Ave. South
Minneapolis, MN
55415

Dear Minnesota Twins,

I want to be your mascot - THE MINNESOTA TWIN. I come out and I
have a mechanical "twin" that duplicates every movement I do.
People love it! I dance around, move about, run, stop, start,
tumble. The mechanical twin makes every move I do.

I could enter the field during the 7th inning stretch or just
flail around on the sidelines between pitches. I would sprint,
gallop, flutter, flap, twist, AND shout, and do the wave. It's up
to you.

Please let me know who I can show my "Minnesota Twin" routine to
when I arrive in Minnesota. Should I just come to the stadium?
And who do I talk to about being your new mascot? Thank you.

Sincerely,

Ted L. Nancy

Ted L. Nancy

MINNESOTA TWINS

1987 & 1991 World Champions
1965 American League Champions

1/9/96

Ted L. Nancy
560 No. Moorpark Rd. #236
Thousand Oaks, CA 91360

Dear Mr. Nancy,

Thank you for your interest in the Minnesota Twins. Our mascot position has been filled for the 1996 season. However, if you would possibly like to perform in our new plaza area outside the dome please contact me at 612-375-7463 (This would be a non-paid area).

Also, when and where will you be in the Twin Cities?

Cordially,

Brian P Brantley

Brian P. Brantley
Game Production Coordinator

560 North Moorpark Rd #236
Thousand Oaks, CA 91360

Executive Offices
MINNESOTA VIKINGS
9520 Viking Dr.
Eden Prairie, MN 55344   Dec 14, 1995

Dear Minnesota Vikings:

I was told I needed to get permission from you to do my
"Minnesota Viking" in my performance piece on nationwide
television.

I am dressed as a Minnesota Viking. I wear a Viking outfit -
horns, leather shorts, spear, woolly skin, open toe shoes - but
talk like a Minnesotan and make references to living in
Minneapolis. (The snow, shivering, bobsledding). This is a
positive upbeat portrayal of a Minnesota Viking. There are no
vulgarities, no profanities. Although I do make one small obscene
gesture, but only as part of a poem. I am a long time fan of the
Minnesota Vikings so I would do nothing that would even be
considered disparaging as far as the logo goes. Remember, this is
on television.

So, I need to secure permission from you to do this portrayal
before I can do the television show. Thanks, Minnesota Vikings.
Please let me know as soon as you can. The show is at the end of
January. Appreciate it.

Sincerely,

Ted L. Nancy
The Minnesota Viking

MINNESOTA VIKINGS

9520 VIKING DRIVE • EDEN PRAIRIE, MN 55344 • (612) 828-6500

December 20, 1995

Ted L. Nancy
The Minnesota Viking
560 North Moorpark Rd. #236
Thousand Oaks, CA 91360

Dear Ted,

Thank you for your letter requesting our permission to do your "Minnesota Viking" performance piece on nationwide television.

However, without a little more information, we cannot give you the permission you seek. We would like to see a video preview of your performance so we can see the context of the use of "The Minnesota Viking".

The Vice President of Marketing, Stew Widdess, would also like to talk to you about your performance. You can reach him at 612-828-6500 ext. 245.

Please contact us at the above number or mail us a video with your phone number attached and we will contact you.

Sincerely,

Lois E. Martens

Lois E. Martens
Executive Assistant to the
Vice President of Marketing

lm

12-11-95
Ted L. Nancy
560 N. Moorpark Rd. #236
Thousand Oaks, Ca. 91360

American College of Sports Medicine
P.O. BOX 1440
Indianapolis, In 46206

Dear American College of Sports Medicine,

I am a kinetic engineer with an interest in "surgically enhanced athletic performance."
I believe it is possible to increase an athlete's performance by surgically modifying his or
her body. The following procedures are the ones I wish to pioneer:

Amphibulation (Am-fib-u-la-shun)-- By webbing a swimmers hands, a good swimmer
could become a world class athlete. Is this any different than an actor receiving hair
plugs to increase his potential? If actors can get hairplugs why can't I make my hand
bigger?

Extentiadigitation (Ex-ten-sha-dij-a-ta-shun) By elongating a swimmer's fingers he can
reach the finish line .015 seconds quicker – sometimes the difference between first and
second place. Or fifth and sixth.

Podialongation (Po-dee-all-long-a-shun) – Adding several inches of bouncy flesh to the
sole of the foot will increase a basketball player's leaping ability and reach, allowing him
to become a better rebounder. Is this any different than an exotic dancer receiving breast
implants to get better jobs?

I will only focus on these three for now. MY QUESTION: Is there anyone currently
practicing these types of procedures, and can you please direct me to any (plastic)
surgeons interested in working in a now-forming sports clinic specializing in
performance enhancement surgery?

I thank you in advance for your assistance. Please direct me in the right direction.

Sincerely,

Ted L. Nancy

AMERICAN COLLEGE
of SPORTS MEDICINE ₅ₘ

January 9, 1996

Dear Ted:

Thank you for contacting the American College of Sports Medicine. Unfortunately, we do not have dispensable information on the subject you requested.

The American College of Sports Medicine, headquartered in Indianapolis, is the largest sports medicine organization in the world, with nearly 15,000 members involved in science, medicine, education and sports.

We do have a monthly journal entitled **Medicine and Science in Sports and Exercise (MSSE)** which contains clinical studies and original investigations. Additionally, each year there is a supplemental issue containing over 1200 presentation abstracts from the ACSM Annual Meeting. This is probably the best place to check for the information that you have requested. It is available in any medical library or most large public and university libraries.

In addition, you may consider contacting the American Council on Exercise at Tel.: (619) 535-8227.

Thank you for thinking of ACSM. Good luck.

Sincerely,

Dave Ferrell
American College of Sports Medicine

Street Address: 401 W. Michigan St. • Indianapolis, IN 46202-3233 USA
Mailing Address: P.O. Box 1440 • Indianapolis, IN 46206-1440 USA
Telephone: (317) 637-9200 • FAX: (317) 634-7817

1996 ANNUAL MEETING — MAY 29-JUNE 1 — CINCINNATI, OHIO

560 No. Moorpark Rd. #236
Thousand Oaks, Ca 91360

Administrative Offices
EMERSON COLLEGE
100 Beacon Street
Boston, MA 02116

Jan 13, 1996

Dear Administrative Offices:

I was told that you are seeking my services to speak at the
Emerson College Student Union on March 8, 1996.

<u>To describe myself:</u>
I have been hit by lighting 6 times. Twice in the head, once in
the back, three times on the rest of my body. I speak about what
it was like to be out for 20 minutes, lifted off the ground, and
in a state of electrical panic. I also speak about how for 2 days
I thought my name was Mark. And, what it was like to visit the
other side half a dozen times. In my candid talk, I tell what
it's like to be the only man in America to have survived 6
lightning attacks. There is one man in England that has been hit
more. I make a reference to him in the talk.

I also talk about my problems incurred at the result of lightning
hitting me behind the ear. Double vision, night sweats, a rash.
Also, what it was like to fall off a building. I was told that
you wanted my speaking services for the evening of March 8th.

Thank you, Emerson. Please contact me and let me know what
housing you have secured for me. Also...I CANNOT be around any
coffee makers. I must make my travel arrangements soon, so please
write and let me know what time my talk is on the 8th and who I am
to meet to take me there. Thanks.

Sincerely,

Ted L. Nancy

EMERSON
COLLEGE

100 BEACON STREET BOSTON, MA 02116-1596

Ted Nancy
560 No. Moorpark Rd. #236
Thousand Oaks, CA 91360

January 23, 1996

Dear Mr. Nancy:

We received your letter dated January 13, 1996 which is attached. We have found no records at the college of any plans to sponsor your talk. We will be making no further arrangements.

Emerson College Student Union

560 No. Moorpark Rd. #236
Thousand Oaks, CA 91360

2/16/96

Submissions Department
HIGHLIGHTS FOR CHILDREN MAGAZINE
2300 West 5th Ave
PO Box 16278
Columbus, OH 43216

Dear Submissions Department:

I have a freckle on my back, that when I stretch, looks like
Anthony Quinn. I would like to sell my back as part of a magazine
article. People love to look at my freckles. Should I send in
the picture of my back for your magazine? Obviously I can't sell
my back. Can I?

I have a few other freckles on my arm and a mole that when bunched
together kinda looks like Richard Gere. When not bunched, Andy
Griffith. If I brush the gray hair over the mole it looks like
Gere. No gray hair, Andy Griffith. As I look at it now in the
light, it looks like Andy Griffith.

Do you want to see it for your magazine? It would look good on
your "fun" page. Who should I send the pictures to? Everyone
always asks me to show them my freckles and moles. (And
blemishes). The doctor said with age, as the freckle bleaches
out, it could look like Dick Van Patten. I really enjoy your
magazine. I am a long time reader. This is just a fun thing with
these freckles. So, please let me know if I should send in a
picture of my back and arms for your magazine. Thanks very much.

Sincerely,

Ted L. Nancy

Editor
Kent L. Brown Jr.

Coordinating Editor
Rich Wallace

Senior Editors
Tom White
Christine San Jose, Ph. D.

Science Editors
Jack Myers, Ph. D.
Andrew Boyles

Associate Editors
Christine French Clark
Allison Lassieur
Marileta Robinson
Jean K. Wood

February 29, 1996

Dear Mr. Nancy:

Thank you for proposing to send pictures of your freckles
to *Highlights*. Based on their descriptions in your query, we
feel that they would not meet *Highlights'* needs at this time.

We appreciate your interest in *Highlights for Children*.

Sincerely,

The Editors

Ted L. Nancy
560 North Moorpark Rd. #236
Thousand Oaks, California
91360

GENERAL MANAGER
GUTHRIE THEATER
725 Vineland Place
Minneapolis, Minnesota
55403   Jul 15, 1995

Dear Sir:

I am interested in speaking with someone regarding staging a
production of my play prior to its Broadway run. (Dates
secure).

The play is a one man show: "JAMES WHITMORE IS HAL HOLBROOK."
And it deals with the esteemed actor's life in his portrayal of
one man shows. I would need to hire a local crew and possibly
some talent if the play is opened up. (May be by the time of
booking).

I would need the theater for a total run of seven (7) weeks but
I can be slightly flexible with this. I would also need a
parrot which I can secure in your area.   And I would need a
suitable dressing room for the actor who is playing James
Whitmore.

Please direct me to the person that I may speak with regarding
financial details: how much the charge would be for rent of your
theater, hiring of your local crews, renting costumes, bee
wranglers, etc. I would also need to know if your prop
department carries certain props: a medicine ball and a dental
chair.

Hal Holbrook has had an great career playing one man shows: Mark
Twain, Herbert Hoover, Teddy Roosevelt,etc. Now we give this
great actor a glossy tribute to his own life.

Hoping to speak with you soon, I remain...

Your friend in theater,

Ted L. Nancy

THE GUTHRIE THEATER

GARLAND WRIGHT
ARTISTIC DIRECTOR

EDWARD A. MARTENSON
EXECUTIVE DIRECTOR

July 28, 1995

Ted L. Nancy
560 North Moorpark Road #236
Thousand Oaks, CA 91360

Dear Mr. Nancy:

I write in reference to your letter of July 15. Unfortunately, the Guthrie Theater is available for one-day rentals only. Long-term rentals are not possible given our own busy performance schedule.

I am sorry that we are unable to accomodate your request. I wish you the best of luck with your production.

Sincerely,

Lendre

Lendre Kearns
Communications Director

VINELAND PLACE, MINNEAPOLIS, MINNESOTA 55403 (612) 347-1100

560 No. Moorpark Rd. #236
Thousand Oaks, CA 91360

Submissions Dept.
STAR MAGAZINE
660 White Plains Road
Tarrytown New York 10591   Jan 29, 1996

Dear Star Magazine:

I have a corn on my foot that resembles Shelley Fabares. How can
I get my corn submitted to your magazine for inclusion? This is a
standard size corn that closely resembles the "Coach" star. When
I turn my foot in the light, the resemblance is uncanny. You
would think Shelley Fabares is on my foot. (Can be mistaken for
Ellen Degeneres if looked at fast. Buy why)?

My podiatrist said he will take off this corn soon. He says it is
not healthy to keep a corn on your foot that long, even if it
looks like a celebrity. I'd like to let the world see it before
it is removed. How can I do this? Please let me know how I can
send in the picture of my corn that looks like Shelley Fabares?
Thanks.

Sincerely,

Ted L. Nancy
Ted L. Nancy

660 WHITE PLAINS ROAD • TARRYTOWN • NEW YORK • 10591 • 914 332-5000

February 6, 1996

Dear Writer:

Thank you for your recent submission to STAR. We have reviewed your material and we're afraid it is unsuitable for our publication - but it was good of you to think of STAR.

I'm sure you'll understand that the volume of mail we receive makes it impossible for us to answer each submission individually with a more detailed critique.

Good luck in placing your story.

Sincerely,

Phil Bunton
Editor

THANK <u>YOU</u>!

A BIG THANK YOU
IS CERTAINLY IN
ORDER

Ted L. Nancy
560 No. Moorpark Rd..#236
Thousand Oaks, CA 91360

Jul 13, 1995

Customer Relations
BALLYS HOTEL AND CASINO
3645 Las Vegas Blvd So.
Las Vegas, Nevada 89109

Dear Customer Relations Dept:

I would just like to say what a pleasant experience your
HOUSEKEEPING DEPARTMENT was during my recent stay.

Usually people have complaints about maid dervice but I want to
PRAISE the fine men and women of Housekeeping. Every day there
were fresh towels and sheets in my room.

The housekeeping people were courteous in respecting my "Do not
Disturb" or "Now For Maid Service" sign on my door.

One day, the minute I had turned my sign over from "DO NOT
DISTURB" TO "MAID SERVICE PLEASE" the cleaning gal was right
there. There wasn't a wait of 15 seconds before she was at my
door with her ammonias and washcloths. It was like she was like
a big cat outside ready to prance at the moment my sign was
turned around.   My room was cleaned within moments and I was
free to start messing it up again by 10:30 in the morning.

Thank you, BALLYS, for a most wonderful experience in the maid
department.

The Housekeeping staff was the most efficient I have ever seen.
I asked for clean towels on a daily basis and they were there.
There was always soaps and toilet paper and shampoos. Every
day. I also noticed that small soap slivers were not removed
but put aside on the tub. (VERY GOOD!) I use these!

Thanks Again,

Ted L. Nancy

BALLY'S.
LAS VEGAS

FRITZ UEBLER
Vice President-Hotel Operations

August 12, 1995

Mr. Ted L. Nancy
560 No. Moorpark Road, #236
Thousand Oaks, CA   91360

Dear Mr. Nancy:

Thank you so much for your letter which I received on
July 20th in which you informed us how pleased you were
with our Housekeeping Department.

A copy of your letter has been forwarded to our Director
of Housekeeping so she can share the accolades on her
staff.

It is truly delightful to receive such a nice letter,
and I want you to know we really appreciate it. If I
can ever be of any assistance to you in the future, please
feel free to contact my office.

Sincerely,

Fritz Uebler

FPU/jr

Copy: Kay Weirick
       Director of Housekeeping

560 N. Moorpark Rd. #236
Thousand Oaks, Ca. 91360

GENERAL MANAGER
MGM GRAND HOTEL & CASINO
3799 Las Vegas Blvd So.
Las Vegas, NV 89109   Aug 4, 1995

Dear General Manager, Sir:

In a world of people always complaining, sometimes it's nice to
STOP and single out a department for EXEMPLARY BEHAVIOR. I am
talking about your CAB STAND CALLERS. I was a frequent visitor to
your hotel last week many, many times. It seems that every night
for almost a week I was at your hotel gambling. Slots, Keno, Pow
Gai, Poker, Roulette (won on this), 21, Dice.

Every time I came out of the hotel to leave for any reason your
fellas running the CAB CALL STAND would go through a complete
military type drill to secure me a cab. They would blow their
whistle a short shrill, move their right arm fast, get that cab
moving towards me. In general, making sure I had a taxi cab and I
had it almost the minute my feet hit the outside pavement.

In a world of slow moving people this DEPT. was fast, fast fast.
My cab was right there ready for me to be whisked away as soon as
I gave him the cab "nod:" I come out of the hotel, move my head,
he moves his head in recognition and the whole cab rolling to the
curb operation begins: Come out of hotel - move head - cab caller
nods at me - he blows whistle, moves arm - cab moves up.) Then he
opens the door, smiles at me, tells the cab where I am going. He
did everything but put a whisk broom on me. I think this is the
most incredible service. It's a person making sure another person
is being properly taken care of by still a another person. All
strangers. Thank you, MGM GRAND, for this most unbelievable
experience. (No more Showboat!)

Please let me know that the CAB STAND DEPT. was thanked. It is
very important to ME that I KNOW that THEY KNOW that SOMEONE has
appreciated THEIR dedication to YOUR hotel. These were courteous
men (and WOMEN). They deserve a little recognition! One fella
was almost hit by a cab. I noticed him rubbing his elbow when I
looked back. Thanks again for making my experience at the MGM
GRAND a GREAT ONE!!!

All the best,

Ted L. Nancy

September 12, 1995

Mr. Ted L. Nancy
560 N. Moorpark Rd. #236
Thousand Oaks, CA 91360

Dear Mr. Nancy:

Please accept my thanks for the compliments you extended to us during your recent stay at the MGM Grand Hotel. I would particularly like to thank you for commending us on the outstanding service our cast members exhibited and provided. A copy of your letter will be forwarded to the Hotel Operations where the Cab Stand department will be recognized.

The staff of the MGM Grand is committed to providing unmatched grand class service. As we strive to attain that goal, we understand the importance of every guest's point of view.

Thank you for taking the time to write and letting us know that we are doing a good job.

Sincerely,

Priscilla Coogle
Customer Service Specialist
(702)891-3386

560 N. Moorpark Rd. #236
Thousand Oaks, CA 91360

Customer Relations
BALLY'S HOTEL & CASINO
3645 Las Vegas Blvd. So.
Las Vegas, NV 89109   September 7, 1995

Dear Bally's,

I had a very nice experience in your hotel last week and I
thought you should know about it. I am talking about your
COFFEE SHOP BUS STAFF. I was so impressed with your hotel and
this group of people that I had to sit down and compliment you.

I visit Las Vegas often. I always try and visit Bally's when I
come to Las Vegas. I definitely feel Bally's is the best place
to gamble. Last week I had the occasion to find myself at
Bally's five or six times during the week. There was a group of
us and whenever anybody said "Where do you want to go?"
everybody chimed in "Bally's."

I had a most pleasant experience with your coffee shop bus boys.
These were courteous, fine young people who cleared away my
dirty dishes immediately after enjoying a meal. Cups,
silverware, saucers, cigarettes, dirty napkins - all cleared
away as soon as I nodded my head. I HAVE NEVER SEEN THIS KIND
OF QUICK SERVICE BEFORE. These fine people were at my table
almost immediately and I did NOT have to wait LONG before my
area was policed and I was ready to start ordering a desert or
whatever. (And messing up again).

In a world of people not caring I thought this group should be
SINGLED OUT for meritorious service. And complimented. I bet
not too many people compliment the bus boys; I think they
deserve a pat on the back every now and then.

Please let me know that the bus staff was thanked. This is very
important to me. These fine employees make a hotel like Bally's
proud to be in. You better believe that cleanliness and getting
your dishes away quick is important to a visitor. Don't you
like your dirty dishes cleared right away? Thank you, Bally's,
for making my many times in your coffee shop a great time before
I started my gambling fun. Your bus staff is the best that I
have ever seen. They deserve recognition. Thanks

Sincerely,

Ted L. Nancy

BALLY'S.
LAS VEGAS

FRANK RIGLEY
Assistant Vice President-Food and Beverage

October 4, 1995

Ted L. Nancy
560 North Moorpark Rd. #236
Thousand Oaks, CA 91360

Dear Mr. Nancy:

Thank you for taking the time to write to us about your pleasant experience in our Coffee Shop. Your very complimentary comments regarding our bus personnel will be shared with my staff so that they appreciate that friendly and professional service is recognized by our guests.

Thank you again for your loyal support and patronage.

Sincerely,

FRANK RIGLEY
ASST. VICE PRESIDENT - F&B

FR/dr

560 N. Moorpark Rd. #236
Thousand Oaks, Ca. 91360

Sept. 6, 1995

GENERAL MANAGER
SANDS HOTEL & CASINO
3355 Las Vegas Blvd So.
Las Vegas, NV 89109

Dear Sands General Manger:

It's not often in this fast moving, steam ahead, world that we really get the chance to stop and compliment someone. In a world of fastly moving people sometimes it's just nice to single out ONE EMPLOYEE who SLOWED DOWN and made your stay more comfortable.

I am talking about the MAITRE'D at your George Wallace show. I had a special vinyl easy chair (Art Linkletter brand) that this fine young man accommodated me with. He removed the chair that was at the table and had MY CHAIR put in its place so I could watch the show on my chair. (I only needed help with the cushions. Bellhop carried.) Although this took time and a few people had to be moved about, this MAITRE'D was most gracious at every moment maneuvering my oversized chair around the aisle and jockeying people around. He listened to no one's comments around him. Eventually everyone was squeezed in.

And he would TAKE NO GRATUITY for this. He simply commented that it was his pleasure to assist me with this chair. And there was concern when he thought he ripped the vinyl but he did not. He examined the area very carefully! He did bang (slice?) his elbow. He was grimacing when I left the show in the middle to use the facilities. There was more help here with the chair in and out of the aisle; more people's comments.

In a world of PEOPLE WHO DON'T CARE - this very nice gentleman was most courteous, elegant, and caring. I would not hesitate to come back to the Sands again and see shows and gamble all night. (I am changing from The Showboat). Please thank this Maitre' D (I don't know his name. But I believe he is the Upper echelon Maitre 'D that the others work under. I did see him bark at the others). Please let me know if he was properly thanked. This is important to me because he was so gracious. Thank you very much!

Thanks again.

Nancy
Coming to Vegas since '88

September 23, 1995

Mr. Ted L. Nancy
560 North Moorpark Road
Thousand Oaks, CA 91360

Dear Mr. Nancy:

A copy of your recent letter was forwarded to my office. I like to encourage guests
to write us their comments. It it especially nice when these comments are in
positive form. I am pleased to know that one of our employees made your stay most
pleasurable. I am glad to know you enjoyed the show and that we were most
accommodating to your needs.

It is pleasing to know that you are considering staying at the Sands Hotel on your
next visit to Las Vegas. We are looking forward to serving you in the future!

Sincerely,

Phillip E. Barnett
Vice President of Food & Beverage
Sands Hotel Casino

cc: A.Waltzman
PB:ro

560 N. Moorpark Rd. #236
Thousand Oaks, CA 91360

VICE PRESIDENT AL GORE
Admiral House
34th And Massachusetts
Washington, D.C. 20005

Jul 15, 1995

Dear Mr, Vice President,

I think you are the best Vice President this country has ever
had!   I think that you bring a certain something to the Vice
Presidency that hasn't been there before.   There are many of us
out here that admire the work you do. We know you care about
us.

So even though we don't tell you every day that we think you're
doing a great job this note says THAT YOU ARE!!!

I hope you are Vice President forever! You're more than a VP -
you're an MVP - Most Valuable Vice President.   I could see you
as Vice President for-ever!   Under many Presidents.   You look
like Sylvestor Stallone. Same hair. God bless the work you do!

With utter respect,

Ted L. Nancy

THE VICE PRESIDENT
WASHINGTON

August 18, 1995

Mr. Ted L. Nancy
560 North Moorpark Road #236
Thousand Oaks, California 91360

Dear Mr. Nancy:

Thank you for writing to me. I am overwhelmed by the many letters and cards I have received from people, like you, who have committed themselves to positive change in America.

As you know, the President and I are making every effort to meet the challenges facing our country in a positive and responsible manner. Your active participation and your continued support are essential to the success of our efforts.

I am genuinely grateful for your kind words of support and encouragement. I look forward to working with you to create a better future for this great nation.

Sincerely,

Al Gore

AG/mrm

560 North Moorpark Rd.
Apt #236
Thousand Oaks, Ca 91360

PRESIDENT
PURINA DOG CHOW
Checkerboard Square, St. Louis, MO
63164

Dear Sir:

I am a happy Dog Chow user for years. My dog, "Cinnamon" is 26
years old (no kidding!) and she's been kept on Purina the whole
time. Except for the beginning when she was on a dog food that
she didn't like!

I would like to know if you make a Purina chow food for senior
dogs? My vet can't belive she's this old but he has her birth
records. He scratches his head every time I bring her in. June
22, 1971, born in St. Petersburg, Fla. No zip back then.

He says she could easily live another four years. It's only 48
months, he says. That would make her 30 and the oldest dog he's
ever seen! But "Cinnamon" is doing great and we love her! He
says that her diet is the best. That's what's keeping her up.
I tell him it's Purina. He says that's because Purina is the
best.

I just wanted to tell the president of Purina Dog Chow about my
(almost) 30 year old dog. And his dog food that keeps her
going.

Thanks for years of great dog food. I'm for Purina all the way!

Sincerely,

Ted L. Nancy

Jul 12, 1995

Ralston Purina Company

Grocery Products Group
Office of Consumer Affairs

July 26, 1995

Mr. Ted L. Nancy
560 N Moorpark Road
Thousand Oaks, CA 91360

Dear Mr. Nancy:

We are happy to hear that throughout her long life, Cinnamon has enjoyed
Purina Dog Chow and would like to thank you for your nice comments.
Your taking the time to write us is very much appreciated.

Unfortunately, in this day and age of hectic life-styles, individuals
don't always take the time to send thank you or complimentary letters to
other individuals, much less a large company, such as ours. Believe me,
we are very pleased you thought of us.

We have enclosed some information about our dog food products which we
hope will assist you in determining which product might be best suited
for your dog's particular needs. We would suggest that you share this
information with your veterinarian as your veterinarian is in the best
position to examine your dog and determine if your she has special
dietary needs.

If you decide to change your Cinnamon's present diet, we recommend that
you add a small amount of the new product gradually increasing the new
product and reducing the current product you're feeding until she is
totally on the new Purina product. This changeover should take
approximately seven to ten days. By changing your her diet in this
manner, we would not expect any intestinal problems to occur.

As an expression of our thanks for writing, we'd like you to accept the
enclosed coupons to use with future purchases of Purina products. Don't
hesitate to contact us at any time should you feel we can be of any
assistance to you.

Sincerely,

Jill R. Barry
Consumer Representative

Checkerboard Square
St. Louis, Missouri 63164-0001

FNF 30561B-94A2

GOIN' PLACES

**I'M SORRY, BUT WE DON'T HAVE THE EQUIPMENT
YOU ARE NEEDING TO WALK ACROSS THE ROOM.**

...SHOWBOAT INN MOTEL

Ted L. Nancy
560 No. Moorpark Rd. #236
Thousand Oaks, CA. 91360

GREYHOUND BUS COMPANY
350 North St. Paul
Dallas, Texas 75201   Aug 31, 1995

Dear Greyhound Bus People:

I have a situation which I would like to address to you and get
your approval on. I was told to write to the corporate offices
after I inquired about this to one of your ticket personnel.

I am part of a traveling dinner theater group. In noticing my
itinerary for our performances I realized that I will be exiting
your bus with little time to spare to get to the theater. This
is on about five different cities. Therefore, I will have to
stay in costume throughout my bus ride so I can make it to the
theater in time. I WILL NOT HAVE TIME TO EXIT THE BUS, CHANGE
INTO COSTUME, AND GET TO THE THEATER ON TIME.

I will be dressed like a giant stick of butter. That is the
costume I wear. I did not want to alarm the other passengers,
or your employees when I check in dressed as a large butter. I
play Morris, the Giant Butter in this exciting new play about
the food industry.

The costume is completely flexible; it bends when I sit in your
comfortable cruiser seat. Once seated, I will look like any
other passenger (except for the top of my head which is a square
yellow piece about 4 inches higher than a normal head). It's
only when I use the restroom that other passengers will notice a
giant butter walking down the aisle.

I cannot change in the bus as I need help in getting the butter
costume on. (Over 57 buttons). I therefore would have to check
in dressed like a giant butter and board the bus this way. I
would exit the bus dressed in my costume so I can make it to the
performance on time. What do you think? Can I get approval
for this? I have always heard that Greyhound Bus Lines goes out
of its way to please its passengers. This would surely help me.
Otherwise I would have to cancel this play because I simply
could not get dressed in time. I need this work!

Thank you, Greyhound, for being a company that cares about it's
riders. I am anxious to get my (19 city) tickets now.

Respectfully,

Ted L. Nancy

OCTOBER 2, 1995

TED NANCY
560 N MOORPARK RD APT 236
THOUSAND OAKS, CA 91360

GREYHOUND LINES, INC
PO BOX 660362
DALLAS, TEXAS 75266-0362

REF: 0000095173

Dear Mr. Nancy:

Thank you for expressing your concerns about the situations you may encounter while using our services. On behalf of Greyhound Lines, I would like to advise you there should be no problem traveling while in your butter costume.

In case of any incidents, please carry a copy of this letter with you in reference to the approval of this situation. If any problems occur you may also contact our Customer Service Department at 1-800-822-2662 during the hours of 7:00AM - 7:00PM CST and your file can be accessed to acknowledge your special circumstances during travel.

We look forward to servicing your needs in the future, and wish you the best of luck with you play and your future in the entertainment industry. Thank you for allowing Greyhound the chance to service your special needs for the duration of your play.

Sincerely,
Bob Morrow
Customer Assistance Analyst

560 North Moorpark Road #236
Thousand Oaks, Ca 91360

Sept. 6, 1995

AMERICAN HAWAII CRUISES
550 Kearny St
San Francisco, CA 94108

Dear American Hawaii Cruise Executives,

I, and my companions, would like to book a cruise on your
American Hawaii Cruises. We are planning our fall cruise
schedule now. We are three (3) Gentlemen traveling (friends
only) that are considered a group for traveling purposes. But
not a group for other purposes. Our problem: We have a
disability that I would like to bring to your attention.

Myself, and my 3 companions * suffer from Tourettes Syndrome. We
have the highest level, the most severe form of the disease.
Let me tell you it's not easy. There can be embarrassments from
this at times.

I can control the disease in written communication by using the *
key when I feel the urge to spew out a slew of loud obscenities.
Vocally, I can not. When traveling we try to be in areas that
are the least embarrassing to this situation. Like around
elders, etc. But it's not always easy.

I would appreciate any courtesies you can give myself and my
fellow travelers regarding what we can do/or expect regarding the
shouting of obscenities. I have always enjoyed American Hawaii
Cruises from hearing about them. It is * the kind of cruise I
would like to go on. We all need to get away a little.

Please let me know, American Hawaii, ** what can be done to
possibly control the situation. (At least let the crew know).

If you feel, this would disrupt your cruise (some people are
going on a romantic cruise, so I can understand) then we'll
arrange some other form of Fall enjoyment. I can understand
your position. We'd love to take our cruise. Thank you.

Sincerely,

Ted L. Nancy
Ted L. Nancy

AMERICAN HAWAII CRUISES

September 20, 1995

Mr. Ted L. Nancy
560 North Moorpark Road
#236
Thousand Oaks, CA 91360

Dear Mr. Nancy:

I am in receipt of your letter dated September 6, 1995.

I am pleased to know that you and your travelling companions are
considering American Hawaii Cruises for your fall vacation. However, I
regret to inform you that our sailings for the remainder of 1995 are currently
full.

Thank you for your inquiry.

Cordially,

Linda Heckman
Vice President-Passenger Services

LH/bb

MAINLAND OFFICE
TWO NORTH RIVERSIDE PLAZA, CHICAGO, ILLINOIS 60606-2606 • 312.466.6000 • FAX 312.466.6001
S.S.CONSTITUTION • S.S.INDEPENDENCE

560 No. Moorpark Rd. #236
Thousand Oaks, CA 91360

Reservations
THE BOULDERS RESORT
PO Box 2090
Carefree, AZ 85377   Dec 6, 1995

Dear Reservations Desk:

I would like to check in to your resort but I have an affliction I
need to address to you. I am considered a level 4 bed wetter.
Although in six months I will be reclassified a level 3. I am
also a heavy sleeper. I take MANY naps during the day. What can
I expect in the way of assistance in this area?

I am sorry I have this. Believe me, it's been a real problem for
me. I try to deal with it the best way I know how. I am an adult
(56 years old) and this is an embarrassing situation. I like to
let the hotel know so that I don't damage anything. (Plants,
dresser, etc.).

I chose your resort because of the service I know you give guests
that wet their bed AND because of the city you're in: Carefree.
(Is that the same as the gum)? I thought you would be receptive
to my problem. I want to come for 6 days.

Can you provide me with a bed wetting sheet, or should I bring my
bed wetting kit? This is MY rubber sheet, twist ties, mattress
pads, disinfectants.

Thank you, Boulders Resort for getting back to me on this. I
appreciate any concern you can give me in this area. Let me know
as soon as you can as I have to secure my reservations. Also...do
you have smoking rooms?

Sincerely,

Ted L. Nancy
Ted L. Nancy

THE BOULDERS

December 18, 1995

Mr. Ted L. Nancy
560 No. Moorpark Road #236
Thousand Oaks CA 91360

Dear Mr. Nancy,

Thank you for your recent correspondence and your request for information and accommodations at The Boulders. I sincerely appreciate your concern regarding advising us of your condition and want you to know that we will do everything possible to maximize your comfort while staying with us. We take pride in our ability to handle special requests and upon learning of your confirmed reservation will secure the necessary supplies to accommodate your needs. I am afraid that I did not understand your comment regarding damage to plants or furniture that might occur due to your condition. I would appreciate if you could advise me of what steps we might take to reduce the risk of this happening.

We do allow smoking in our guest rooms, however it is not permitted in our dining facilities. If I can be of further assistance please do not hesitate to contact me directly. We look forward to seeing you soon.

Sincerely,

Rick Houston
Resort Manager

RH/tf
encl.

560 No Moorpark Rd. #236
Thousand Oaks, CA 91360

Jan 24, 1996

Reservations Dept.
BEVERLY HILLS HOTEL
9641 Sunset Blvd.
Beverly Hills, CA 90210

Dear Reservations Dept:

I am 2 feet 3 inches tall and appear around the world as "Pip The
Mighty Squeak."

MY QUESTION: I want a room at your hotel for the week of Feb 21-
28. Because of my size, I need to know if special accomodations
can be arranged for me? I am very tiny.

I need a 3 foot bed and a dresser that's only 1 foot high. (So I
can reach). Also, do you have a shower head that is 30 inches off
the floor? A regular shower head blows me all over the tub.

I know these are unusual expectations but sometimes I can be
accommodated. It's tough, but it can happen if the hotel is
equipped for micro people. My act consists of me in a teacup held
by a giant. That is how small I am.

I have traveled throughout the world as "Pip The Mighty Squeak,"
an act like no other. I stop and start in many directions. Some
hotels have small furniture and beds. One even had a tiny soda
machine!

So, let me know if I can be accomodated for the week of Feb 21. I
need to make my reservations now, so please let me now if these
dates are available. Thank you for your prompt reply.

Sincerely,

Ted L. Nancy
Pip The Mighty Squeak

January 31, 1996

Mr. Ted L. Nancy
560 North Moorpark Road #236
Thousand Oaks, CA 91360

Dear Mr. Nancy,

Thank you for your interest in The Beverly Hills Hotel. We do have universal access rooms available for the requested dates.

These rooms are equipped with hand held shower heads that have moderate water pressure. Although we do not carry 1 foot high dressers, the dressers in the rooms are very low and spacious. The beds in the guest rooms are slightly over 6 feet, however, we are confident that our concierge will be able to assist you in locating a smaller bed for your room at the lowest cost possible to you.

We have enclosed a brochure including our room rates for your perusal. Our universal access rooms are in the deluxe guestroom with balcony or suite category only. If you would like to make a reservation, please call us at 1-800-283-8885. As we have a 24 hour cancellation policy, we would need a credit card to guarantee the reservation.

If we can be of further assistance to you, please do not hesitate to contact us.

Sincerely,

Barbara M. Manix
Reservations Manager

560 North Moorpark Road
Townhome #236
Thousand Oaks, California 91360

Reservations
WOODMARK HOTEL
1200 Carillon Point
Kirkland, Washington 98033   Sep 5, 1996

Dear Reservations,

I wish to make a reservation for your fine hotel for 2 nights, Oct
6th and 7th. I want to explain a situation which I want to make
you aware of.

I travel with 2200 red ants. Although these are loose ants, they
will be kept ONLY in the hotel room. All 2200 red ants will be
accounted for and NONE will leave the hotel room or be left in the
room. I will keep all sweets tied with a twist tie bag.
(Including pretzels). They will not venture far away from the
bags. Trust me.

These ants ARE NOT pets, so your NO PETS rule should not apply. I
travel with these ants for a reason. I watch them. It calms me
down. I watch for hours as they work, then I am refreshed and
ready to go. I like watching them moving about the room. They
carry a crumb across the room and I watch this. It has a very
calming effect on me and helps me with my business.

You'd be surprised what a conversation piece over 2000 ants can be
during a business meeting. When I have a business visitor to my
room on Oct 6th or 7th we will both watch these ants then get down
to business.

I will describe these red ants to you. They are 1/16th of an inch
long, and weigh less then 1/10th of an ounce per handful. They
are reddish with some spotting, and have ant features. I do not
drink, I don't smoke, I don't take drugs. (Once a mushroom). I
have red ants to relax me. Please confirm with me my reservation.

Thank you,

Ted L. Nancy

The
WOODMARK HOTEL
on Lake Washington

Mr. Ted L. Nancy
560 North Moorpark Road
Townhome #236
Thousand Oaks, CA 91360

Dear Mr. Nancy,

Thank you for your letter regarding a reservation for October 6th and 7th. Unfortunately we will not be able to accommodate your arrival on those dates. Due to our location along the water, and the season, we regularly fumigate the carpets of the rooms and corridors.

Thank you for considering The Woodmark Hotel.

Sincerely,

Laura Weertman
Reservations Manager

560 North Moorpark Rd. #236
Thousand Oaks, CA 91360

THE DELTA QUEEN STEAMBOAT CO.
30 Robin Street Wharf
New Orleans, Louisiana
70130-1890   Nov 29, 1995

Dear Delta Steamboat:

I will be arriving by ferry soon and I would like to book passage
on a Delta Queen Steamboat cruise. I am very impressed with your
brochure and from what people tell me about your magnificent
vessel. LOU!!!

I have an affliction which sometimes makes traveling uncomfortable
and I think you should know about it so we can figure out how best
to handle it. I have a barking disease. Level 4. I can control
most obscenities but the shouting goes in cycles, themes.
Sometimes, it's a slew of obscenities, sometimes just vulgarities.
I am truly sorry. I wish it wasn't this way but I must deal with
it. For the past 14 months I bark out men's names. I cannot
control this. I can control some of the things I bark out. I no
longer yell out full obscenities. But now this is the shape the
disease takes.

In writing, which is the way I prefer to communicate in public, I
can control the urge by writing down the name when I feel the urge
to spew. Will this be a problem? I can understand people not
wanting to be around someone yelling. I know it's uncomfortable
for all when folks are strolling, having a quiet, romantic
evening, etc. I do take medication which controls a lot, but I
prefer to communicate with my writing pads. However, I do want to
take the steamboat cruise to relive the days of Mark Twain, and
his jumping frog. So...I hope this won't be a problem to other
seagoers.

Please give me information so that we can discuss where I can
stand on the boat so as not to affect the most people. FRED!!!!
Thank you, Delta Steamer. Many people have taken your cruises and
reported back as to how much they enjoyed it. I'd like to take
your cruise. I am anxious to sail. STEVE!!!!

Hey, thanks again. Please send me info: times, schedules,
clothing, food servings, cabin arrangements, etc. I am waiting.
MARK!!!!

Sincerely,

Ted L. Nancy

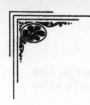

December 7, 1995

Mr. Ted L. Nancy
560 North Moorpark Rd. #236
Thousand Oaks, CA 91360

Dear Mr. Nancy:

I have received your letter of November 29, 1995. Yes, you are indeed welcome aboard our vessels and we will do all we can to make things comfortable for you. It is kind of you to be considerate of others. There would not be a public place we could say none of the other passengers would go, but you could decide if you wanted to leave an area. The only place that would be private, is one of our cabins with a private veranda. This might be something you'd like to consider. Certainly, we would be glad to book you in any cabin you choose.

Communicating through writing on board would not be a problem. When you are ready to book, a travel agent would be helpful, and we will document your reservation so the boat is ready to accommodate you in every way possible.

You mentioned you have our brochure, if you have any further questions, please contact us and we'll be happy to help you with your Steamboatin' adventure.

Yours very truly,

Anne Wall
Anne Wall
Manager, Individual Reservations

AW/ba

The Delta Queen Steamboat Co.
30 Robin Street Wharf · New Orleans, Louisiana 70130-1890
Local (504) 586-0631 · Fax (504) 585-0630

9-26-95
Ted L. Nancy
560 N. Moorpark Rd. #236
Thousand Oaks, Ca. 91360

Manager
RITZ CARLTON HOTEL
160 East Pearson Street
Chicago, Ill. 60611

Dear Ritz-Carlton,

I will be making reservations soon to stay overnight at your hotel. During my visit I will
be involved in several very important meetings in your bar area and restaurant with
potential investors.

As part of my presentation, I will be checking in and taking my meetings dressed as a
ripe banana. Business decisions will be based on my presentation, and I must be certain
that while meeting in the bar area and restaurant I am left undisturbed by curious patrons.
Perhaps a booth in the back? I don't mind mingling with people in the foyer or lobby.

I look forward to your reply regarding my privacy when dressed as a banana, and a
mutually prosperous stay.

Sincerely,

Ted L. Nancy

THE RITZ-CARLTON
Chicago
A FOUR SEASONS · REGENT HOTEL

Robert D. Cima
Hotel Manager

October 6, 1995

Mr. Ted Nancy
560 North Moorpark Road, #236
Thousand Oaks, California 91360

Dear Mr. Nancy,

Thank you for your note inquiring about your privacy during your future stay at The Ritz-Carlton, Chicago.

I am pleased that you had forewarned us in regards to the ripe banana costume. I must let you know that the basic attire in the hotel is formal. A costume being worn will be viewed as unacceptable for our hotel. However, we would be delighted in assisting you to arrange a more private meeting space.

If you would like to proceed with a reservation here at The Ritz-Carlton, Chicago, please contact us as soon as possible so we may assist in the details.

Sincerely,

CITY HALL WEST HOLLYWOOD
OFFICE OF THE MAYOR
8300 Santa Monica Blvd.
Los Angeles, CA 90069-4314   Aug 10, 1995

RE: INK SPOT STOCK

Dear Mr. Mayor:

I had heard that you were sponsoring in your beautiful city of
West Hollywood the event "THE INK SPOTS DAY" On Sept 27, 1995.
I understand this is an all day fair honoring the Ink Spots and
their contribution to American song.

How can I get fair tickets and what is the lodging like that
time of year?   I have long been a fan of the Ink Spoits and
want to take part in this great celebration.

I think it's a wonderful idea to have an entire day built around
the Ink Spots. "INK SPOT STOCK." I heard that there will be
many food vendors, portable johns, and possibly the group itself
will be signing autographs. Will all the Spots be there for the
entire event?

Please send me information (Weekend package, hotel parking, hand
stamping, etc.) on "INK SPOT STOCK."

West Hollywood is a beautiful city. It's what America is about.
Quiet, wholesome, good tuna melts. Thanks for putting on this
great event. It means a lot to some of us.

Respectfully,

Ted L. Nancy
560 N. Moorpark Rd., # 236
Thousand Oaks, Ca. 91360

City of West Hollywood
California 1984

CITY OF WEST HOLLYWOOD

CITY HALL
8300 SANTA MONICA BLVD.
WEST HOLLYWOOD, CA
90069-4314
TEL (213) 848-6460
FAX (213) 848-6562

CITY COUNCIL

JOHN HEILMAN
Mayor

PAUL KORETZ
Mayor Pro Tempore

SAL GUARRIELLO

ABBE LAND

STEVE MARTIN

September 20, 1995

Ted L. Nancy
560 N. Moorpark Rd., #236
Thousand Oaks, CA 91360

Dear Mr. Nancy:

Thank you for your letter of August 10th. Unfortunately this is not a West Hollywood sponsored event and we are unaware of the program.

The Ink Spots are a favorite of mine. If you find out any more details, please let us know.

Very truly yours,

John Heilman

John Heilman
Mayor

JH:lf

Ted L. Nancy
560 No. Moorpark Rd. #236
Thousand Oaks, CA. 91360

ALOHA AIRLINES
P.O. Box 30028
Honolulu, Hawaii 96820   Aug 31, 1995

Dear Aloha Airlines People:

I have a situation which I would like to address to you and get
your approval on. I was told to write to the corporate offices
after I inquired about this to one of your ticket personnel.

I am part of a traveling dinner theater group. In noticing my
itinerary for our performances I realized that I will be exiting
your airplane with little time to spare to get to the theater.
This is on about five different cities. Therefore, I will have
to stay in costume throughout my plane ride so I can make it to
the theater in time. I WILL NOT HAVE TIME TO EXIT THE PLANE,
CHANGE INTO COSTUME, AND GET TO THE THEATER ON TIME.

I will be dressed like a giant rotting radish. That is the
costume I wear. I did not want to alarm the other passengers,
or your employees when I check in dressed as a large radish. I
play Angelo, the Rotting Radish in this exciting new play about
the food industry.

The costume is completely flexible; it bends when I sit in your
comfortable seat. Once seated, I will look like any other
passenger (except for the top of my head which is a round red
piece about 4 inches higher than a normal head). It's only when
I use the restroom that other passengers will notice a giant
radish walking down the aisle.

I cannot change in the plane as I need help in getting the
radish costume on. (Over 157 buttons). I therefore would have
to check in dressed like a giant radish and board the plane this
way. I would exit the plane dressed in my costume so I can make
it to the performance on time. What do you think?   Can I get
approval for this? I have always heard that Aloha Airlines goes
out of its way to please its passengers. This would surely help
me. Otherwise I would have to cancel this play because I simply
could not get dressed in time. I need this work!
Thank you, Aloha, for being a company that cares about it's
passengers. I am anxious to get my (19 city) tickets now.

Respectfully,

Ted L. Nancy
Angelo, The Rotting Radish

AIRLINES

Daniel S. Gleason
Staff Vice President
Passenger Sales

901 Waikiki Trade Center
2255 Kuhio Avenue
Honolulu, Hawaii 96815
Facsimile 808 926-0442
Telephone 808 923-9622

September 11, 1995

Mr. Ted L. Nancy
560 N. Moorpark Road, #236
Thousand Oaks, CA 91360

Dear Mr. Nancy:

In response to your letter of August 31, 1995, we will need to know which Aloha Airlines flights you plan to take. Could you please provide me with that information?

While we generally do not set any criteria on our passengers' dress, safety may be an issue. In the case of an emergency, the rotting radish might impede a rapid egress from the aircraft of yourself and other passengers. If the possibility of this exists, then we would probably be unable to accept you in costume. I do not know how we can evaluate this without a visual inspection; could you please also send us a photo of Angelo.

As soon as we have the above information, we will be able to answer your question.

Sincerely,

/gb

560 No. Moorpark Rd. #236
Thousand Oaks, Ca 91360

Jan 24, 1996

Reservations
DISNEYLAND HOTEL
1150 W. Cerritos Ave
Anaheim, CA 92802

Dear Reservations:

I would like to stay at your hotel for one night on February 24th.
I would like to know if I can check in with my own ice machine?

This is a standard size hotel ice machine. Five feet high and
three feet wide. It constantly makes ice. (As soon as I plug it
in). (There is NO dripping). I can carry it to the room by
myself. I need NO help in getting it through your lobby and into
my room. This will allow me to have fresh ice in my room without
having to go to the hallway for it. This ice machine leaves no
water mark on your carpet.

My reservation will be for Feb 24th. I also may want tickets to
Disneyland. So, please let me know if I can check in with my own
ice machine and bring it to the room on that date. Thanks for
getting back to me on this as I have to make my reservations NOW.
This is a business trip.

Sincerely,

Ted L. Nancy

Disneyland Hotel

February 4, 1996

Mr. Ted L. Nancy
560 No. Moorpark Rd. #236
Thousand Oaks, CA 91360

Dear Mr. Nancy

We are delighted that you will be staying with us on February 24th. Although one of our primary goals is to ensure that your stay with us is a pleasant one, we cannot accommodate an ice machine in any of our guest rooms. The Disneyland Hotel is equipped with ice machines on every floor, and can be accessed at any time by our guests. If you prefer to have ice brought to your room, room service would be happy to accommodate you (for a nominal fee).

If you have any other questions or concerns, please contact the reservations department at (714) 956-6400, or the Disneyland Hotel operator at (714) 778-6600. We are looking forward to having the opportunity to serve you. Thank you for choosing the Disneyland Hotel!

Sincerely,

Debbie Beardsley

Debbie Beardsley
DLH Reservations Assistant Manager

560 North Moorpark Rd
#236
Thousand Oaks, CA 91360

2/1/96

Reservations Desk
SHOWBOAT INN HOTEL
660 N. Virginia St
Reno, NV 89503

Dear Showboat Inn Hotel:

I want to register as a guest at your fine hotel, Mar 5, 1996,
but have a predicament that must be addressed.

I have recently lost my balance. I usually walk with a balance
dog, but in the room I will be alone. I may look tipsy when I
walk, but I have just lost the use of my balance, that's all. (In
room I use a balance bar - similar to high rope walker). Can I
get furniture that has no sharp corners?   Dressers and beds
should have round corners. Also what about mirrors? I have my
own.

Do you provide for the balance disadvantaged? My heels are not as
round as the bottom of my feet. I had heard that your hotel was
set up for this. Believe me it's not easy. I may look like I'm
falling down, but I'm only balance disadvantaged. Thanks for
getting back to me on this. I want to make my reservation now so
I can come to your beautiful hotel and see shows, gamble, and move
about the room. I may appear like I'm slipping, but this is just
my malady. Thanks for letting me know if the March 5th date is
"ok." Also...do you have smoking rooms?

Sincerely,

Ted L. Nancy

SHOWBOAT INN

660 N. VIRGINIA · RENO, NEVADA 89501
TELEPHONE: (702) 786-4032

2/6/96

Mr Ted L. Nancy
560 North Moorpark Rd.
Thousand Oaks, CA 91360

Dear Mr. Nancy —
Thank you for your letter inquiring about our Motel — However, since you refer to us as a Hotel and mention shows, Gambling etc I feel you are wanting a Hotel. We are a large Motel, No Restaurant & No Casino — We are within walking distance of several large Hotel Casinos. I'm sorry, but we do not have the equiptment you are needing to walk across the room. We are the only Showboat Inn in Reno, but there is a Showboat Hotel & Casino in Las Vegas & Atlantic City — We are not connected with these Hotels — This is an independly owned Motel.

Sincerely,
Kathryn Lennon, Mgr

Ted L. Nancy
560 No. Moorpark Road #236
Thousand Oaks, Ca   91360

Reservations Desk
PAN PACIFIC HOTEL SAN FRANCISCO
500 Post Street
San Francisco, CA 94012   Jan 24, 1996

Dear Sir or Madam:

I wish to check-in to your hotel the evening of Feb 21st for three
nights. I have a difficulty that I need to address.

I have three legs. I have two normal sized legs with normal size
feet (size 9 1/2 D) and I have a third leg growing next to my left
leg. This foot is size 12 B. As you can imagine, getting shoes
is very difficult. I have many size 12's that I'll only be able
to wear one shoe. I do not wear shorts!

I'd like to know if you can accommodate me when I check-in to your
hotel? Are there rooms available on Feb 21st? And can a three
legged man be accomodated in your hotel for three days? Also,
I'll need an ottoman I can place next to the bed when I sleep.

Thanks for your prompt reply as I have to make my reservations
now. I have always heard that the Pan Pacific goes out of it's
way to accommodate those with special needs, especially three
legged people.

Sincerely,

Ted L. Nancy

THE PAN PACIFIC HOTEL

San Francisco

Reservations Desk
Pan Pacific Hotel San Francisco
500 Post Street
San Francisco, CA 94012

Ted L. Nancy
560 No. Moorpark Rd.
Thousand Oaks, CA 91360   February 1, 1996

Dear Mr. Nancy,

Thank you for your inquiry regarding our hotel accommodations,
room rates and availability. We do have rooms available
Feb. 21st, for three nights and can offer you our corporate
discount. This rate begins at $215.00 for a superior room
with a queen bed. At the rate of $240.00 there is a deluxe
room which also has a queen bed. And for $265.00 we have a
luxury room with a king bed.

Our rooms do have ottoman chairs in them. If it would help
to accommodate your specific needs, we would be happy to ask
our Personal Valet department arrange to have the ottoman
placed next to the bed prior to your arrival.

If your have any further questions or concerns, please, don't
hesitate to contact us. We can be reached at 1-800-533-6465.
Thank you once again and warm regards.

Sincerely,

Kristen
Reservations Department

At Union Square

500 Post Street, San Francisco, California 94102
Telephone (415) 771-8600, Facsimile (415) 398-0267, Telex 990264

THE PAN PACIFIC HOTEL

San Francisco

Reservations Desk
Pan Pacific Hotel San Francisco
500 Post Street
San Francisco, CA 94102

Ted L. Nancy
560 No. Moorpark 80
Thousand Oaks, CA 91360

February 1, 1996

Dear Mr. Nancy,

Thank you for your inquiry regarding our hotel accommodations,
room rates and availability. We do have rooms available
Feb. 1st, for three nights and can offer you our corporate
discount. This rate begins at $215.00 for a superior room
with a queen bed. At the rate of $240.00 there is a deluxe
room which also has a queen bed. And for $265.00 we have a
luxury room with a king bed.

Our rooms do have ottoman chairs in them. If it would help
to accommodate your specific needs, we would be happy to ask
our Personal Valet department arrange to have the ottoman
placed next to the bed prior to your arrival.

If you have any further questions or concerns, please, don't
hesitate to contact us. We can be reached at 1-800-533-6465.
Thank you once again and warm regards.

Sincerely,

Kristen
Reservations Department

HeY OUT THeRe!

it's Me

560 No. Moorpark Rd. Apt 236
Thousand Oaks, CA 91360

Sep 11, 1996

Tickets
LOS ANGELES LAKERS
PO Box 10
Inglewood, CA 90306

Dear Los Angeles Lakers,

I want to buy a ticket for your next home stand. Go Lakers!
Because of my injury, the backside of my pants must be completely
cut out. A cellophane wrapper is replaced in that area causing
complete exposure. I CAN get a doctors note if you want. I don't
want to cause a disturbance at the game, but I do want to jump up
out of my seat and yell for the Lakers.

The only time you will see my cellophane exposed buttocks will be
during the time I enter and exit the arena and during behind the
back passes and 3 point buzzer shots.

In essence my backside is cut out with cellophane over it. I have
seen cowboys with this look in line dancing so it's not too bad.

How much is a ticket? I hope my see through rear end will be
acceptable at your next home stand. Let me know about the
doctor's note.

Sincerely,

Ted L. Nancy

1972 · 1980 · 1982 · 1985 · 1987 · 1988
WORLD CHAMPIONS

September 18, 1996

Mr. Ted L. Nancy
560 N. Moorpark Rd., #236
Thousand Oaks, CA 91360

Dear Mr. Nancy,

If you are concerned that your exposure is an embarrassment our assumption would be that you can find some way to drape or cover yourself. Especially as you are able to walk and jump.   If this is not the case, and you have medical documentation, we will be glad to provide an attendant to escort you to seat and explain your situation to the nearest usher.

Individual game tickets go on sale on Oct. 5 and are priced at $21.00 per game. Once you have obtained your tickets you may give me a call if you feel you need assistance.

Our best wishes to you.

Very sincerely,

Bob Steiner
Director of Public Relations

BS/wp

GREAT WESTERN FORUM
P.O. BOX 10

INGLEWOOD, CA 90306
(310) 419-3100

560 North Moorpark Road
236
Thousand Oaks, California
91360

Manager
MCCORMICK & SCHMICK'S THE FISH HOUSE
206 North Rodeo Dr.
Beverly Hills, Ca
90210   Aug 12, 1996

Dear Sir or Madam:

I would like to dine in your establishment on the evening of
Thursday, Sept 12, 1996.

I have a predicament. I suffer from immense odor. I have tried
everything. Baths, colognes, skin washes. I have been to a
doctor who told me there's nothing he can do. I just stink. It
is embarrassing. I am used to the odor, but I am afraid others
are not.

My question: Can I dine by the garbage area so others won't be
offended? If you can put a table and chair out there I can eat by
your dumpsters. Believe me the smell is that bad. It's stinky!
Everybody will be happy and I'll get my meal. I will sit by your
garbage bins and enjoy my meal. I don't mind the stench

I will pay for any additional expense. It's just that I can't
take the stress anymore and I don't want to offend other diners.

I have been successful with this at other restaurants but to tell
you the truth I am SICK OF CHICKEN. I want some good old
fashioned seafood. I have heard of your Copper River salmon. I
write ahead so that when I arrive at your restaurant and you get a
whiff of my odor you won't turn me away. You will simply lead me
to the garbage bins outside and seat me where I will enjoy my
meal.

The reservation will be for Sept 12, 1996. Or another night if
you are busy that night. Let me know. Thanks for writing back.
Again, let me know the cost of this service. Thank you.

Sincerely,

Ted L. Nancy
Ted L. Nancy

The Fish House

September 17, 1996

Mr. Ted L. Nancy
560 North Moorpark Road
#236
Thousand Oaks, California
91360

Dear Mr. Nancy:

Thank you for your second letter of inquiry regarding reservation availability relative to your particular and personal situation. I have received both, and I do apologize for not having responded sooner. I'd like you to know I did try to reach you personally by phone upon receipt of your first letter, but was unable to obtain your number at the Moorpark address.

I must be honest and say your request for seating under the circumstances you suggest is unique to my experience. McCormick & Schmick's has built a reputation on accessibility to all who wish to dine here, but of course even that intention has it's limits based on logistics, liability, and decorum. Accordingly, and although I very much appreciate your consideration of other guests in not wanting to offend them due to your particular condition, your suggestion to seat and serve you in our dumpster area is simply not an option.

We appreciate and agree with your deference to other guests, and indeed have a responsibility to insure that the dining environment at McCormick & Schmick's is pleasant to the general public dining at our restaurants. With that in mind, the only possible option may be a reservation in our conference room on our mezzanine level dining room. This option would of course be subject to the room's availability, and typically it is booked for a minimum number of people (10 - 15) because it entails dedicated service by one waitperson.

Having reviewed the above, and with the intention to satisfy your request, we would have to discuss the matter directly to insure that all potential details are covered. I would be happy to have that conversation with you either by phone, or in person, at your earliest convenience.

Please feel free to call me at your convenience. My schedule as a Senior Manager has me visiting our three Los Angeles restaurants on a weekly basis. Please try any one of the following numbers, in the order presented. Should I be in a meeting, please inform the host that I requested to be interrupted for the call. I look forward to speaking with you soon.

Beverly Hills   310-859-0434
Downtown L.A.   213-629-1929
Pasadena   818-405-0064

Until then, yours very truly,

Gary Nellis
Senior Manager

Two Rodeo • 206 N. Rodeo Drive • Beverly Hills, CA 90210 • Phone (310) 859-0434 • Fax (310) 859-7106

560 No. Moorpark Rd. #236
Thousand Oaks, CA 91360

Jan 12, 1996

Executive Offices
SHASTA SODA
PO Box 4617
Hayward, CA 94540

Dear Shasta Cola,

I had heard you were changing your name to Laarksvard's Hot Cream.
Why? I have enjoyed Shasta strawberry soda for years, why change
now? This will only confuse your many Shasta strawberry drinkers.

I have always asked for your soda by saying, "Shasta, please. May
I have a Shasta strawberry soda?" I don't think the name
changeover will be easier for me to remember. Some of us can't
remember those unusual names. I would rather say Shasta
strawberry soda them Laarksvard's. (And forget that hot cream).
Shasta strawberry tastes best ice cold. Everyone knows that!
Also, Shasta cola is the perfect amount of syllables to say when
asking for a cold one.

So, please, Shasta strawberry, tell me that you are keeping the
name "Shasta strawberry soda" and not changing it to Laarksvard's
Hot Cream. Thanks for your response regarding this matter. I
need to know!

Only A Shasta Strawberry Sipper,

Ted L. Nancy

Shasta Beverages Inc.   26901 Industrial Boulevard
Hayward, California 94545

Telephone 510. 783. 3200   Executive Offices

January 25, 1996

Ted L. Nancy
560 No. Moorpark Road, #236
Thousand Oak, California 91360

Dear Mr. Nancy:

Thank you for contacting Shasta Beverages and sharing your concern
regarding Shasta Beverages changing it's name. Shasta Beverages
is owned by National Beverage Corporation and we are not changing
our name to Laarksvard's Hot Cream. We appreciate you taking the
time to inquire about this name change and for sharing your
concern with us. I hope this will put your mind at ease to know
we will continue to be **SHASTA BEVERAGES CORPORATION**.

Shasta has been in the beverage business since 1889, and we are
proud of our company's long history and commitment to producing
good tasting, thirst-quenching products.

Enclosed please find complimentary Shasta coupons toward your
family's next purchase. It has been a pleasure to serve you.

Sincerely,

Martha Fleming
Consumer Relations

(NANCY)

cc: D. Gorden/La Mirada
     B. Halsey
     N. Eichberger
     J. Caporella
     D. Thompson/Duluth

MR. BOB ARUM, TOP RANK, INC.
(BOXING SHOWS)
ESPN
ESPN Plaza
Bristol, CT.   06010

Dear Mr. Arum:

I know that many heavyweight fighters are aging but still
fighting. Evidenced by the 46 year old George Foreman winning
the championship.

But I was just appalled at the recent news that a planned
Schmeling-Holmes fight is in the works. What is going on here?
I deplore you, Mr. Arum, do not let this happen. Max Schmeling
has to be 85 years old. Has everyone gone insane?!

How can an 85 plus man living in Germany properly train to fight
an athlete of Larry Holmes' formidable skills. Larry Holmes is
still in decent shape and this fight will be a disgrace! He
will knock Schmeling out in the FIRST ROUND!!! I have seen
Larry Holmes fight and he is still a finely tuned athlete.
Hell, James J. Corbett was 38 when he challenged.

Something must me done to stop this aging in sports. I suggest:

A.) When an athlete reaches 30 he is immediately reclassified.
He must sign in and have his signature verified at Macy's (or
another large building capable of holding many).

B.) Double the cornermen in each fighter's corner. (We need
safety) 2 cornermen, 2 cutmen, 2 assistants, 2 men to pour water
on the fighters hair and sponge him off. The cornerman is
allowed to hold the fighter up in the ring until his senses are
gone or his eyes are glazed.

I beg you, Sir, not to allow this fight. Max Schmeling should
lead a dignified life as a Coca Cola executive in Germany. Not
a heavyweight contender. Do you think Coca cola should still
advertise? Don't you think everyone has heard of this product?

Thank you for years of good clean boxing. You are the best at
bringing great fights into people's lives.

Ted L. Nancy

Top Rank, Inc
3900 Paradise Road, Suite 227
Las Vegas, Nevada 89109

Tel 702-732-2717
Fax 702-733-8232

August 9, 1995

Mr. Ted L. Nancy
560 N. Moorpark Road, Apt #236
Thousand Oaks, CA   91360

Dear Mr. Nancy,

Thank you so much for your letter of July 12 which I just
recently received. The points made in your letter are very
valid.

Indeed, I immediately took steps to prevent this event from
ever taking place. I can tell you now that due to your valid
concern, any plans to put on this event have been abandoned.

Mr. Schmeling will be able to ease into his nineties without
the risk of serious bodily harm.

The executives of HBO as well as the members of the Nevada
State Athletic Commission were all very supportive in helping
me kill the project.

Thank you for your prompt notice.

Sincerely,

TOP RANK, INC.

Bob Arum

560 N. Moorpark Rd. Apt #236
Thousand Oaks, CA 91360

Jul 12, 1995

AMERICAN FOREST AND PAPER ASSOC.
260 Madison Ave.
New York, N.Y. 10016

Dear Paper People:

I got your name from other paper bag enthusiasts in my area. We
need to get back to the good old days when you got just a paper
bag after your supermarket purchase. There was no choice - none
of this "paper or plastic" crap. I am so sick of that! I can't
listen to that paper or plastic b.s. anymore.

We need to get back to the old days when the paper bag was our
only choice. There are too many choices in America today.

It's the same with cigarettes: menthol, non menthol, filter, no
filter. Hell, one cigarette, one man. Isn't that enough? How
many cigarettes can you smoke? Isn't that the question!?

Let's just campaign to keep the paper bag the only choice you
have in the supermarket. It will clear up a lot of garbage
(both figuratively and literally) in this universe. One bag,
one people. Besides, plastic bags clog the blow-holes of whales
and dolphins!!!.

Let me know what you think. I would like literature about your
organization. I support paper sacks. Get back to basics! Am
awaiting your reply.

Thanks for keeping this in the public's eye,

Ted. L. Nancy

July 19, 1995

Mr. Ted. L. Nancy
560 N. Moorpark Rd., Apt. #236
Thousand Oaks, CA 91360

Dear Mr. Nancy:

I appreciated your letter of July 12, 1995. It is not often that we receive such
enthusiastic support for the paper bag!

Currently, the Paper Bag Council, a committee of the American Forest & Paper
Association comprised of paper company executives, is hard at work on a paper bag
campaign. Our goal is to increase the reuse and recycling of paper bags. With this
goal in mind we hope people like yourself will realize the paper bag's many benefits
to our environment.

Also, we appreciate your concern for marine life. We want you to know, in light of
the destruction caused by plastic bags to our oceans, beaches and marinelife, that
many environmental groups strongly support the use of paper bags.

Enclosed please find some materials which I hope you will find helpful. Once again,
thank you for your interest.

Sincerely

David C. Stuck
Manager
Paper Bag Council

enclosure

American Forest &
Paper Association
1111 19th Street, NW
Suite 800
Washington, DC 20036
Phone: (202) 463-2422
Fax: (202) 463-5189

Ted L. Nancy
560 No. Moorpark Rd., Apt 236
Thousand Oaks, Ca.   91360

Nov 29, 1995

Product Development Dept.
THE UPJOHN CO.
Kalamazoo, MI 49001

Dear Development Dept:

This is my second letter!!   <u>MY QUESTION:</u> Who comes up with the
product names? I mean who's job is it to think of the names you
give your drugs?   Who thinks of the name Motrin?   And the name
Mentadent?   And Gyne-Lotrimin, and Triaminicin? It all sounds
like Jerry Lewis gibberish. "Gynalotriminnnn!!! Dynahabanene!!"
These names are just a bunch of made up names and really don't
mean anything, do they?   I mean when they say "Now new Micatin
has Miconazole."   You made up the name Micatin AND you made up
the name Miconazole. You could have said Micatin has Nibbitin
and it would have been the same thing. Because Miconazole is
just something you named up in your lab. Isn't it?

I have a product called Jidgebin. How can I get this product
considered at your company for distribution? I am a long time
salve and ointment developer as well as a fungus customer.   I
believe this product will help eliminate fungus. I'd like to
show it to someone in research there. How do I do this? Should
I just send it in?

It's a blessing that a big company like yours grows and make this
a better America. The UPJOHN COMPANY. A great American company!

Thanks for your help. I have used your ear drops for years!

Respectfully,

Ted L. Nancy

PHARMACIA & UPJOHN, INC.

301 Henrietta Street
Kalamazoo, MI 49001-0199

Arthur R. Diani, Ph.D.
Senior Technology Assessment Specialist
Acquisitions Review and Contracts (7223-24-322)

TELEPHONE: (616) 385-4510
TELEX: 901-240-1468
FACSIMILE: (616) 385-7207

December 12, 1995

Ted L. Nancy
560 North Moorpark Road
Apartment 236
Thousand Oaks, California 91360

Dear Mr. Nancy:

Thank you very much for your letter of 11-29-95 in which you inquire about the origin of trade names for drugs and the process by which your antifungal, Jidgebin, could be evaluated by Pharmacia & Upjohn, Inc. to determine our interest in a possible acquisition. First, trade names for our drugs are developed by a Corporate Trademark Committee through input from Marketing and Legal representatives. A trade name search is conducted by Legal to ascertain that the prospective trade name is not confusing or similar to other trade names already in use. The prospective trade name for a drug to be marketed in the United States is then submitted to the FDA for final approval. Second, with respect to your antifungal, Jidgebin, it is doubtful that we would have interest at this time. Since it appears that Jidgebin is a topical antifungal, this opportunity does not represent a good fit with our discovery strategy or business plans for infectious diseases.

Thank you again for your interest in Pharmacia & Upjohn, Inc. and we wish you success with the further development of Jidgebin.

Sincerely yours,

Arthur R. Diani

Arthur R. Diani, Ph.D.

Ted L, Nancy
560 N. Moorpark Rd #236
Thousand Oaks, Ca 91360

July 11, 1995

CUSTOMER SERVICE MANAGER
ROBINSONS-MAY DEPARTMENT STORE
6160 Laurel Canyon Blvd
No Hollywood, Calif
91606

Dear Robinsons-May Customer Service Manager:

I was in your store the other day and I was paying by check.
When I started to write the check out, the sales clerk asked me
if I had another form of identification.

I told her I did and pulled out a credit card with my name on
it. It was at this point that I started thinking: Your store is
relying on me to tell you it's me. I mean you want me to verify
for your employees that it's me.

I'm thinking they don't know me, don't know my check, yet
they're relying on me to tell them it's me. Shouldn't there be
a third party involved here? Preferably from your side. Don't
you think you should have someone involved from your end?

This is not a complaint. I am very happy with Robinsons-May and
have shopped there for some time.

This is about an identification system that is teetering on
insanity.

When you ask a stranger to tell another stranger that they can
verify it's them - then you are asking for at least one person
to tell you they're not them. They will be lying to you.

I think a better system would be this: While they are shopping
you can run a signature check through the Department Of Motor
Vehicles and get their mother's maiden name. Then when it's
purchase time - verification is complete. What do you think of
this idea?

Thank you for your time,

Ted L. Nancy

ROBINSONS·MAY

A DIVISION OF THE MAY DEPARTMENT STORES COMPANY

EXECUTIVE OFFICE

July 14, 1995

Ted L. Nancy
560 N. Moorpark Rd. #236
Thousand Oaks, CA 91360

Dear Mr. Nancy,

Thank you for your recent correspondence regarding our bank check acceptance policy.

The forms of identification that we request for customer check approval are requirements set by an outside agency which we employ.

Your comments are very much appreciated, as it is through communication from our customers that we may be made aware of any opportunity to improve. We will forward your opinion of our bank check policy to our Senior Management staff for their review.

Again, thank you for writing and thank you for shopping at Robinsons♦May.

Sincerely,

ROBINSONS♦MAY

Kristin Ness
Manager, Customer Service

KN:ian

7-25-95
Ted L Nancy
560 N. Moorpark Rd. #236
Thousand Oaks, Ca. 91360

Senior Management Staff
Robinson-May Dept. Store
6160 Laurel Canyon Blvd.
North Hollywood, Ca. 91606- 3247

Dear Senior Management Staff,

Recently, Kristin Ness forwarded to you a "check and credit card security procedure" I recomended for the Robinson-May department stores. (A great place to shop!) I am happy you are running with my idea, and while it is still being discussed, I'd like you to consider several more suggestions.

First, upon entering the store, and at locations around the store, a person planning a purchase with a credit card OR check, would leave their signature and fingerprint on a laser pad, patched directly into your verification hub, which would be linked up to the Department of Motor Vehicles or the Registrar of Voters.. By the time they've reached the checkout counter, you've already had them VERIFIED and CONFIRMED..

Also, you could also offer discounts to Robinson-May credit card holders who agree to the following security measures:

When applying for credit, in front of an authorized employee, a customer would be required to remove a clump of their hair. The hair's imprint and personal DNA code would be stored in Robinson-May's security system. When the consumer is ready to make a purchase, he lays his head on a protein imprint-analysis scanner, approving or declining the purchase based on his remaining credit or checking account balance. The cost savings on the reduction of forgery, fraud, etc., will more than offset the cost of the system. Trust me, the technology is there, and I know where it is.

I look forward to your reply.
I will always shop at Robinson-May -- you have the fewest pins in your shirts.

Sincerely,

Ted L. Nancy

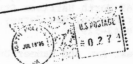

SANTA ANA CA
JUL 19 '95

U.S POSTAGE
$ 0.27⁴

Ted L. Nancy
560 N. Moorpark Rd. #236
Thousand Oaks, CA 91360

91360-3700 B⁸

Ted L. Nancy
560 N.Moorpark Rd.
Apt 236
Thousand Oaks, Ca 91360

Jul 12, 1995

Consumer Relations Dept.
ARM & HAMMER BAKING SODA COMPANY
Div of Church & Dwight Co., Inc
469 North Harrison Street
Princeton, New Jersey
08543-5297

Dear Arm and Hammer Deodorant People:

I visited your Arm & Hammer museum in Los Angeles a short time
ago and the only thing I was unhappy about was I found the
museum to be too cold. The air conditioning must have been down
to 40! I was freezing in there!! Something must be done about
this. It spoils the visit when you are so cold you can't enjoy
the paintings because of a veiny headache.

Also...

Is the Picasso that you feature in some of your paintings the
same Picasso that also has the perfume out? I thought since you
also run the deodorant and odor company then perhaps you would
know the answer to this, an obvious odor question.

The museum is beautiful. The art work is sensational, some of
the most impressive I have ever seen. The displays are breath
taking. I was awed.

Also, when I leave your Arm and Hammer baking soda in my
refrigerator for too long my open water container gets a powdery
taste. Anything that can be done about this?

Thanks for a great museum and a great stain remover product! I
will never switch from Arm and Hammer.

Sincerely,

Ted L. Nancy

ARM & HAMMER® DIVISION
CHURCH & DWIGHT CO., INC.
P.O. BOX 826
SPRING HOUSE, PA 19477

1-800-524-1328

September 8, 1995

Mr. Ted L. Nancy
Apt. 236
560 N. Moorpark Road
Thousand Oaks, CA 91360

Dear Mr. Nancy:

We apologize for our delay in responding to you. Thank you for
your interest in our company.

Dr. Armand Hammer was not connected with the ARM & HAMMER®
Consumer Products Division of Church & Dwight Co., Inc. Any
similarity between Dr. Hammer's name and the ARM & HAMMER brand
name is purely coincidental.

Dr. Hammer was named after the character Armand in a play titled
"Camille", by Alexander Dumas. The ARM & HAMMER trademark first
came into use in the early 1860's. It was derived from Roman
mythology and represents the arm of Vulcan, the "God of Fire"
with hammer in hand about to descend upon an anvil.

Dr. Hammer passed away in December, 1990. He was Chairman of
Occidental Petroleum at the time of his death. Although our
Chemicals Division had formed a partnership with Occidental
Petroleum to produce and market potassium carbonate under the
Armand Products name, any shares vested have since been
repurchased by our company.
In addition, If you move the box of ARM & HAMMER® Baking Soda to
another area of the refridgerator, your open water container
should not get a powdery taste. Be sure the baking soda is not
near the fan in your refridgerator or consider using the New
FreshFlo Vents™ Fridge-Freezer Pack™.

We trust this information is helpful. We are enclosing various
leaflets containing further information about ARM & HAMMER
products which we hope you will enjoy. Please contact us again at

ARM & HAMMER® DIVISION
CHURCH & DWIGHT CO., INC.
P.O. BOX 826
SPRING HOUSE, PA 19477

1-800-524-1328

September 8, 1995
Mr. Nancy
Page Two

the toll-free number listed above if we can be of further
assistance.

Cordially,

Regina Lewis
Consumer Relations Specialist

RXL/cl

0201782A

Ted L. Nancy
560 N. Moorpark Rd. #236
Thousand Oaks, Ca. 91360
8/9/95

Jockey Brand Shorts
Kenosha, Wisconsin 53140

To Whom This May Concern,

Wearing Jockey brand briefs has been like a religion with me. I have never worn
anything but. Except for part of '88 when I tried Hanes. Nothing feels like Jockey shorts.

Recently, however, I bought two three-packs of Jockey all-cotton CLASSIC BRIEFS,
and something unusual happened to all six shorts -- they all wore out on the underside of
the crotch (the segment of cloth that runs from just past my testicles to just below my
rear-end).

I have never had this problem before. In the past, they would rip at the waist before any
such hole would appear. My question: Are you treating your briefs in any chemical, or
using a lesser grade cotton in the crotch region? Is it possible I'm swimming in, or using a
soap or detergent that is leaving my testicles more acidic than normal? Have any other
complaints about this problem been brought to your attention. A suggestion: You should
select employees to wash, wear, and monitor the wear and tear of their Jockey shorts, to
make sure someone doesn't get a bad batch of briefs. If anyone should know how
important underpants are, you should.

I look forward to your reply. Jockey brand undershorts are best!

Sincerely,

Ted L. Nancy

Ted L. Nancy

JOCKEY. INTERNATIONAL, INC.

August 18, 1995

Mr. Ted L. Nancy
560 N. Moorpark Road, #236
Thousand Oaks, CA 91360

Dear Mr. Nancy:

Thank you for taking the time to express your concerns about
our products. Rest assured that at Jockey International, Inc.
we strive to fulfill our corporate mission "To provide our
valued customers the highest quality, fashionable and
competitively priced merchandise in the marketplace...products
which guarantee customer satisfaction."

Please complete the necessary information below and return this
completed form. A stamped, self-addressed envelope is included
for your convenience.

Once we receive the information, your replacement merchandise
will be ordered. Please allow three to six weeks for delivery.
We appreciate your patience and hope you accept our apology for
any inconvenience. We hope you will be pleased with your
replacement product.

If we may be of further assistance in the future, please let us
know. We would like you to continue enjoying *Genuine Jockey*
products for years to come.

Sincerely,

Jerry R. Pritchard

Consumer Affairs

Enclosure

Style___9007_____ Color Preference_____

Description of Style_____

Size_____ Qty.___2 pkgs. of 3_____

JOCKEY INTERNATIONAL, INC.,
2300 - 60th STREET, KENOSHA, WISCONSIN 53140 U.S.A. (414) 658-8111

Ted L. Nancy
560 N. Moorpark Rd.
#236
Thousand Oaks, CA 91360

July 15, 1995

GENERAL MANAGER
PORTLAND STAGE COMPANY
P.O.Box 1458
Portland, ME 04104

Dear Sirs:

I am interested in securing your theater for a production of the play: "CINNAMON- A LIFE IN PROGRESS" before it's run on Broadway (dates already secure).

The play needs a tryout arena and I thought your theater would be interested.

The play is about a 26 year old dog and it's bossy owner. We will have six cats each day for rehearsal and a Bee Wrangler during the run of the production.

Please let me know who I would contact to discuss financial arrangements with: Rental of your theater, hiring of local crews, costumes, etc.

A theater such as yours could be the perfect place to have this beautiful play about the lifelong friendship between a dog and it's master. We never see the dog. (We MAY hear a bark).

Thanking you, I remain...

Your friend in theater,

Ted L. Nancy

Ted L. Nancy

560 N. Moorpark Rd., #236
Thousand Oaks, CA.   91360

Jul 15, 1995

DIRECTOR
RADIO CITY MUSIC HALL
1260 Avenue Of The Americas
New York, N.Y. 10020

Dear Sir or Madam:

Is it possible to rent Radio City Music Hall out for the week?

I would be putting on my production of "CINNAMON - A LIFE IN
PROGRESS."   This is a warm hearted family drama.   It has been
playing in the Maine and Minneapolis area.

Now it is ready for NEW YORK.

Please let me know how I would go about renting out Radio City
Music Hall for my production of "CINNAMON - A LIFE IN PROGRESS."

There will be NO Bee Wrangler for these performances.   (May hear
loud barking).

Thank you.   I remain...

Ted L. Nancy

Ted L. Nancy

NO REPLY!

Ted L. Nancy
560 North Moorpark Rd., #236
Thousand Oaks, Ca 91360

COLLEGE GIFTS DEPT.
THE UNIVERSITY OF ALABAMA
P.O. Box 870126,
Tuscaloosca, Alabama
35487-6690   Jul 14, 1995

Dear University of Alabama:

If one wants to leave a gift to a University who does one
contact? I want to bequeath the University Of Alabama a
valuable.

I think Alabama is a fine city; reflecting good clean quality
life in America, morals, sense, and respect and good tuna melts!
I have enjoyed your "Bull Dogs" for ages. I have a valuable
asset that I think the University Of Alabama would make a good
home for.

In correspondence regarding this gift, please refer to
"Cinnamon."

Thank you for your reply,

Sincerely,

Ted L. Nancy

P.S. I think you should build an Alabama Food Hall Of Fame!

THE UNIVERSITY OF ALABAMA

OFFICE OF THE VICE PRESIDENT
FOR DEVELOPMENT

August 2, 1995

Mr. Ted L. Nancy
560 North Moorpark Road, #236
Thousand Oaks, CA 91360

Dear Mr. Nancy:

We are in receipt of your letter regarding what appears to be a proposed gift-in-kind. If you would be so kind to give us more specifics on the nature of the proposed gift, we shall be pleased to provide some details.

Many thanks for your interest in The University of Alabama.

Sincerely,

Larry W. O'Neal
Assistant Vice President

bsf

c   Mr. Hubert Kessler
     Dr. John Scott

560 No. Moorpark Rd., #236
Thousand Oaks, CA 91360

LARRY W. O'NEAL, ASSISTANT VICE PRESIDENT
THE UNIVERSITY OF ALABAMA
284 Rose Administration Bldg., Box 870122
Tuscaloosa, Alabama 35487-0122   August 22, 1996

Dear Mr. O'Neal,

The gift I wish to bequeath to The University Of Alabama are the
remains and memorabilia of "Cinnamon," the world famous 26 year
old show dog. Currently both the Portland Stage Company and
Radio City Music Hall have been notified in an effort to bring
"CINNAMON - A LIFE IN PROGRESS" to the the live stage. The
musical includes a radio-controlled swarm of bees and the
world's largest mobile ecosystem - both theatrical firsts.

"Cinnamon - The World Famous Dog" toured extensively and was a
hit at malls, car washes, multiplexes and European TV, where for
twenty five cents children would pick her up and give her a
squeeze.

The memory of Cinnamon's spirit can be an inspiration to
everyone, as examples can be set by animals as well as humans,
and the essence she embodied would be well served in an
endowment supported shrine. Articles to be included:
Cinnamon's food and water dish (even though she mainly drank
from the pool). Her leash, collar, her special herbal flea
guard recipe. Cinnamon's happy face name tag. Her mattress pad
and rubber sheets. Her Purina letter regarding her as the
world's oldest dog. (And Purina coupons). Pictures and video
of Cinnamon twaddling around. Plus, Cinnamon, herself, stuffed
and scented.

As you can imagine, Cinnamon earned a considerable amount of
money in her long life time. She left quite a large estate.
Perhaps you may be interested in administering this estate?
Please advise as to how I may bequeath this valuable to your
institution. Thanks. I eagerly await your reply.

Sincerely,

Ted L. Nancy
Cinnamon's owner-breeder

STILL WAITING FOR REPLY!

U.S.POSTAGE
$0.32

AUG-3'95

Mr. Ted Nancy
560 North Moorpark Road, #236
Thousand Oaks, CA 91360

560 No. Moorpark Rd. #236
Thousand Oaks, Ca 91360

2/1/96

Special Promotions
FARMER JOHN MEATS
3049 East Vernon Ave
Los Angeles, CA 90058

Dear Farmer John Meats:

I am having a semi small to very large medium <u>fun</u> raiser and would
like to know if I can <u>special order</u> a bologna 59 feet by 22 feet?
We are also giving away a dog.

And what about shipping? Can it be shipped in 2 parts so it
doesn't bend? Or do I have to supply transportation? I think a
very large bologna in a hot truck in the hot sun would probably
not be so good. What do you think? I don't like hot bologna.

Please let me know how much this special order sausage is. (I have
my own roll). I think you have the BEST meat out there. I eat
this stuff up all the time. I weigh 500. I give it as gifts to
postal workers, hedge cutters, messengers, UPS men, massage
therapists. Now, I would like to buy a large bologna for my bi
semi event. Can this be done? Thanks for getting back to me to
let me know if you can make me a 59 foot bologna.

Sincerely,

Ted L. Nancy
Meat Chair Committee

CLOUGHERTY PACKING COMPANY

3049 E. VERNON AVENUE • POST OFFICE BOX 58870

LOS ANGELES, CALIFORNIA 90058-0870 • (213) 583-4621 • FAX (213) 584-1699

U. S. Inspected and Passed Est. No. 360

February 14, 1996

Mr. Ted Nancy
560 North Moorpark Road #236
Thousand Oaks, California

Dear Ted:

Thank you for your letter outlining plans for some fun.

Unfortunately you're going to have to limit the fun to smaller portions. Instead of the planned 59 feet, the longest piece of bologna we can provide is approximately 55 inches. We call this piece of bologna a "slicer". Normally we cut it in half. It's not practical to pack a bologna this large.

However, there is a possibility we could accommodate you. The cost is $1.12 per pound and the slicer weighs approximately 30 pounds.

If you are still interested, call (213) 585-9000, and ask for Mr. George Malone. He will help you with this item.

Thank you for your loyalty to Farmer John.

Sincerely,

Ronald V. Smith
Director of Advertising/Public Relations

RVS:jh

LEADING GOLD MEDAL WINNERS AT THE CALIFORNIA STATE FAIR

Ted L. Nancy
560 N. Moorpark Rd., Apt 236
Thousand Oaks, Ca 91360

July 25, 1995

PRESIDENT
KAL CAN CAT FOOD CO.
Vernon, CA 90058

Dear Kal Can Cat Food President,

I am the happy owner of a 36 year old cat. Unbelievable!! His
name is "Charles" and the vet can't believe it when I bring him
in. But he has his records. (He's been taking care of him the
whole time). He just scratches his head and says this cat has got
to be the oldest cat he's ever seen. He examines him all over.
He was born June 22, 1959. We used to watch Chuck Berry together.
But now his eyesight is bad.

I tell the vet all Charles eats is Kal Can cat food (and sometimes
licorice) but he loves the Kal Can cat food taste. Last week he
examined him and told me that he thought Kal Can makes the best
cat food. He said he tells all his cat owners that if it was up
to him, Kal Can would be the only thing they should serve. Then
he made a strange gurgling sound. He's the best vet!

My question: Is this the oldest cat you have ever heard of? I
thought about taking him around malls and displaying him if he was
the oldest cat ever. I figured you would know being around cats
there all day. Hey, thanks for letting me know. God bless you,
Mr. Cat president. Charles is my companion for life!! What other
cat foods do you make that he should eat? Plese tell me if I
should change to another Kal Can brand. I need to know!

Respectfully,

Ted L. Nancy
(Charles and Me)

3250 East 44th Street • P.O. Box 58853 • Vernon, California 90058-0853 • (213) 587-2727 • FAX: (213) 588-8347

13 September 1995

Mr. Ted L. Nancy
560 N. Moorpark Rd., Apt 236
Thousand Oaks, CA 91360

Dear Ted,

I am delighted to hear about Charles and his amazing longevity. We tried to trace you
by phone, but you are not listed; hence, this letter.

Would it be possible for us to visit you and Charles? I would love to take some
photographs of him for our records. I will also try to track down data on the oldest
recorded cat for you.

Please call me on my direct line, 213-586-4905. I will be looking forward to hearing
from you soon.

In the meantime, please find enclosed some coupons for Charles's continued enjoyment
and health.

Yours sincerely,

John Malin
Vice President
Research & Development

S:\STAFF\MALINJOH\NANCY.SAM

THE FIVE PRINCIPLES

K2252

Ted L. Nancy
560 No. Moorpark Rd.   #236
Thousand Oaks, Ca. 91360

November 29, 1995

Lost & Found Department
COLORADO BELLE HOTEL & CASINO
P.O. Box 77000
Laughlin, NV 89028

Dear Colorado Belle Lost & Found:

I was visiting your hotel recently as part of a semi large to a
full mid size group. We are a considered a group for
entertainment purposes but not considered a group for anything
else. In my visit to your hotel, I was distracted, confused and
lost from the group.

MY QUESTION: I was wondering if you found a bag of hair? This
would be a good size bag of otter hair. I use it as a 2nd coat of
hair for my aging otter. My otter, Louis, is 40. That's 45 human
years.

The hair is grayish - brownish - yellowish with some reddish
striping. It is a hard bristle and has no use except as a 2nd
hair to an otter. Although I have heard of those using it on
their 2nd dog. That is why I am concerned that my bag of otter
hair will end up in the wrong hands. The hair was in a bluish -
greenish bag with a purplish - pinkish name tag clearly
identifying it as OTTER HAIR.

Please let me know If you found my bag of otter hair. I anxiously
await your reply. I have heard that the Colorado Belle goes out
of it way for its guests. Especially when it comes to lost and
found hair. Thanks very much.   I have been coming to the
Colorado Belle loyally for many years. And I will continue doing
so because they have such courteous employees who go out of their
way to make sure their guests are treated fairly. Please let me
know if someone turned in my bag of otter hair? Thank you.

Sincerely,

Ted L. Nancy

Ted L. Nancy

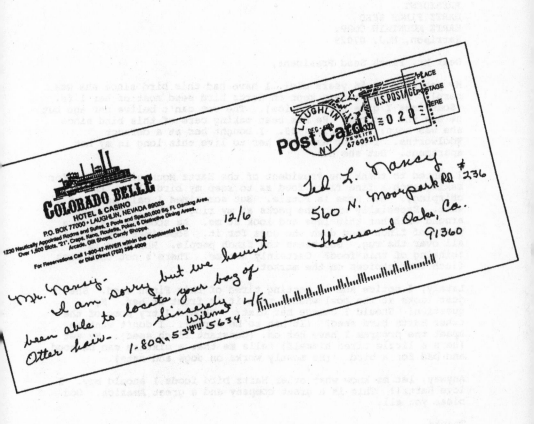

COLORADO BELLE
HOTEL & CASINO
P.O. BOX 77000 • LAUGHLIN, NEVADA 89028
1230 Nautically Appointed Rooms and Suites, 2 Pools and Spa,80,000 Sq. Ft. Gaming Area,
Over 1,500 Slots, "21", Craps, Keno, Roulette, Bingo
Arcade, Gift Shops, Candy Shoppe.
For Reservations Call 1-800-47-RIVER within the Continental U.S.
or Dial Direct (702) 298-4000

Post Card

U.S. POSTAGE
≡ 0.20 ≡
LAUGHLIN
DEC
NV
PB METER
6760521

PLACE
POSTAGE
HERE

12/6

Mr. Nancy —
I am sorry but we havent
been able to locate your bag of
Otter hair —
Sincerely
Wilma
1-809-53rd 5634

Ted L. Nancy
560 N. Moorpark RD #236
Thousand Oaks, Ca.
91360

Ted L. Nancy
560 N. Moorpark Rd., Apt 236
Thousand Oaks, CA 91360

July 24, 1995

PRESIDENT
HARTZ FINCH SEED
HARTZ MOUNTAIN CORP.
Harrison, N.J. 07029

Dear Mr. Finch Seed President,

My pet bird is 56 years old! I have had this bird since she was
born!   And she's been kept on Hartz bird seed most of her life.
(Sometimes I give her licorice). The vet can't belive her age but
he has the records. He has been taking care of this bird since
she was born: June 22, 1939. I bought her at a defunct
Woolworths. I never expected her to live this long in my hot
apartment. But she has.

I wanted to thank the President of the Hartz Mountain Company for
making such a fine finch food as to keep my bird alive. (And
chirping). Her name is Potzie. But sometimes I call her what I
want. Especially when she pecks at my ring. She loves to walk
around with her thin legs and look at me. As soon as I stick a
plate of finch seed down she goes for it. Sometimes she gets it
all over the rug. God bless the finch people. Who else is
thinking of this food? Certainly not me. There's not that much
finch food choices on the market.

Lately, I notice she is getting tired of this Finch seed. She
just looks at the bowl when I push it in front of her. My
question: Should I change her diet?   Should I try some of the
other Hartz bird seed? (It has to be Hartz). I don't want to
upset the program I have her on. (Constant finch seed). My vet
(he's a little tired himself) tells me that a mixture can be good
and bad for a bird. (He mostly works on dogs and cats).

Anyway, let me know what other Hartz bird foods I should buy. I
love Hartz!! This is a great company and a great America. God
bless you all.

Thanks,

Ted L. Nancy

P.S. Are you the same people as the rent a car? "We're number 2."

Patrice Tanaka & Company, Inc.

320 West 13th Street, 7th Floor

New York, New York 10014

Telephone 212 229-0500

Fax 212 229-0523

August 16, 1995

Mr. Ted L. Nancy
560 N. Moorpark Road, Apt. 236
Thousand Oaks, CA 91360

Dear Mr. Nancy,

On behalf of Hartz Mountain, we thank you for your letter regarding your pet
finch, Potzie. We are all quite amazed that Potzie is a 56-year old finch, and
are proud that you attribute Hartz products to her longevity and well-being.

We would be very interested in speaking to Potzie's veterinarian and
receiving copies of his records for Potzie. Kindly call me at (212) 229-0500 or
write to me at PT&Co., 320 West 13th Street, New York, NY 10014 with the
name, address and phone number of Potzie's veterinarian.

Thank you.

Sincerely,

Nancy Rosenblum

Ted L. Nancy
560 N. Moorpark Rd. #236
Thousand Oaks, CA 91360

July 11, 1995

FRITOS SNACK CO.
Dallas, Texas 75235-5224

Dear Fritos:

I have been eating snacks for a long time. I think I have tried
most snacks. Someone told me about Fritos a few weeks ago. I
thought I had tried just about every snack but I had never heard
of Fritos.

Imagine that, in and out of gas station snack shops for a half a
life and I had never heard of this snack.

Anyway, the reason I'm writing is that I opened a bag of FRITOS
and I noticed they were all curled. Every single one of them.
I tasted one, it seemed hard and crunchy. And salty. I threw
the bag away immediately.

You said on the back of the wrapper that if I had any comments
on questions to write FRITOS. So I am writing to you.

Can you please send me a list of other snacks I may not have
tried. Tried Lays Potato chips, and corn curls, Doritos (don't
like the color - so you can cross them off the list!)

I really like snacking so I would love to be a great Fritos
customer!! Send me a list!

Thank you.

Sincerely,

Ted L. Nancy
Ted L. Nancy

August 18, 1995

Mr Ted L. Nancy
560 North Moorpark Road   #236
Thousand Oaks,   CA   91360

Dear Mr Nancy,

Thanks for contacting Frito-Lay.

Enclosed is the information you requested which we hope will be
useful to you. We are pleased to know of your interest in our
products and our company. You are valued as our consumer, and we
hope you will always look for Frito-Lay products whenever you are
looking for great tasting snack foods.

Thanks again!

Sincerely,

Linda Mitchell
Consumer Affairs

Enclosure: 1 Nutrition Book
               1 55 Cents Off Coupon

8830230

560 No. Moorpark Rd. Apt #236
Thousand Oaks, CA 91360

Dec 16, 1996

MR. TIM CONWAY
P.O. Box 17047
Encino, CA 91416

Dear Tim Conway,

I look and act exactly like you. Unintentionally. People that
know me say to me, "Knowing you is like being friends with Tim
Conway." Rest assured I have never done anything to embarrass us.
Even with ugly women. After all, I was me before you was us.

I am sending you a drawing I made. I want to show you how much I
look like you and we look like us. This morning, someone said to
me as I got on the bus with my lunch box, "Hey, it's Tim Conway.
What are you eating for lunch?" I glared and walked to my seat as
he made fun of me for fifty five minutes. (I was having macaroni
and cheese and a sardine).

Would you please sign my drawing of us and send it back? It would
mean a lot to me to know that my idol, the great Tim Conway, has
given me an autograph. I will put it on the wall and look at it.

Thank you very much. I admire your face and height. I look
forward to receiving my drawing back soon.

Keep up the great work on Dorf. I love the tiny feet!

Respectfully,

Ted L. Nancy

Ted L. Nancy

"Us"

Best Wishes

ME!

You

US

EPILOGUE

560 N. Moorpark Rd. #236
Thousand Oaks, CA USA 91360

Jul 18, 1995

KING TAUFA'AHAU TUPOU IV
THE PALACE
P.O. BOX 6
Nuku'alofa, Tonga

Dear King Tupou IV,

I have always liked the name Tonga for a country. The name is
right there. There's no pretense. It's just Tonga.

Have you always been Tonga? Some countries have changed their
name - Iran was Persia - Siam is Thailand. Thousand Oaks used
to be Five Hundred Oaks (expansion - malls, donuts, etc.). I
hope Tonga has always been Tonga. Everybody I mention this name
to likes it.

Also, I noticed your address - the Palace PO Box 6 is the same
as my girlfriend's place of business (she's a dancer at The
Palace on Route 6 (but they use a post office box). Are you
receiving her mail? There may be a mail mixup. She is
expecting medical results back. I was wondering if you have
them?

Is there any picture I could get of you?   Or any picture of
Tonga?   I would love a nice picture of your beautiful country
and I don't know where to get one from. The map store is
closed! (Now a donut store).

   It will be most revered and placed on my wall (The beginning
of my Tonga collection)?

   You are the best. I admire you and your people. Tonga is a
place I'd like to go someday. Do you have any literature?

Tonga Rules!!

Ted L. Nancy

Palace Office,
P. O. Box 6,
Nuku'alofa,
TONGA.
Telephone : 21-000 (676)
Fax   : 24102 (676)

6 Novema 1995

Ted L Nancy
560 N Moorpark Rd.   236
Thousand Oaks, CA
<u>U.S.A.</u>

Dear Ted,

With reference to your letter addressing to His Majesty showing
your interest in our Kingdom we are sorry to say that we don't
have any mail misdelivered.

Enclosed is a photograph of His Majesty, King Taufa'ahau Tupou
IV and Queen Halaevalu Mata'aho and also a brochure which contain
information on our Kingdom with a hope that it meets your
request.

Yours faithfully,

Tupou K Fa'aui
for/Private Secretary
to His Majesty

560 N. Moorpark Rd., #236
Thousand Oaks, Calif. USA 91360

Aug 26, 1996

MR. TUPOU K FA'AUI
For/Private Secretary To His Majesty
KING TAUFA'AHAU TUPOU IV
The Palace
PO Box 6
Nuku'alofa, Tonga

Dear Mr. Tupou K Fa'aui, Sir,

Thank you very much for the brochure of Tonga and the beautiful
picture of the King and Queen. Their military clothes are
splendid. Not garish at all like some countries. Holland are you
listening?

Just one question: In the picture that you sent me, the King is
wearing a beautiful sword at his side. I was wondering whether he
got that sword in Chicago as it looks very much like a Prussian
military sword I lost in the Ritz Carlton bathroom?

Do you think he found my sword? That is where I had it last. In
the restroom. Thank you for letting me know. The swords are very
similar.

I display your picture proudly in my kitchen at home near my
waffle maker. Everyone admires it. (The picture, not the waffle
machine). The King is the ultimate majesty.

Also, when is a good time to visit Tonga? Do you have any
Starbucks there? I like coffee. Have you ever had a Frappacino?
It is cold coffee.

Thank you for getting back to me on this sword thing. Tonga is a
beautiful country. Your brochure really shows off the place. I
hope to hear from you soon.

Respectfully,

Ted L. Nancy

"I BELIEVE THE KING HAS MY PRUSSIAN SWORD."